The Sago Swamp

Richard Masters

A Story of Joy, Despair and Adventure
deep in the Interior of New Guinea

Many chapters are preceded by a traditional tale from many different parts of New Guinea. These are in italics.

30% of the royalties from this book will be shared equally by three charities: Voluntary Service Overseas, Sacred Lands Film Project and Animals Asia.

Richard Masters was born in London. He was educated at Goldsworth School for boys in Woking, George Abbot School in Guildford and at the University of London, Goldsmiths College, where he qualified as a teacher. In 1974 he started his teaching career at Kentwood School for Boys in London and, in 1985, moved to Fairlands School in Cheddar. He has also worked as an estate manager, an actor, an extra in many TV series and a part-time university lecturer at Bath Spa University. He has previously written articles for Times Educational Supplement and others. He now lives in Somerset with his wife Susan and dog Arthur.

This is his second book. The first **As It Should Be** is available on Amazon.

Part One

Yopi lived alone in the forest a few miles from Sugu in the province of Lae. She had a special gift bestowed on her by the moon and the wind. She could speak to any type of animal and understand what they were saying, whether it was a roar, a squeak or a Twitter.

The animals, birds and fish all liked her; she was kind and ate only things she grew in her garden or picked from trees. She never ate meat of any kind.

The two biggest and strongest animals that Yopi knew were the chief of the crocodiles, Cro, and the chief of the wild boar, Bow. They were both very loud and were always telling, whoever happened to be in earshot, about how they were stronger, better looking and cleverer than the other. All the animals and Yopi were tired of hearing their Boasting.

One day, Cro and Bow came to Yopi and demanded that she tell them which one of them was the strongest. She knew she had to be careful, if she chose one, the other would become her enemy and would probably kill and eat her. She told them to come back the following afternoon and then she would tell them.

That night, she thought and thought and came up with a clever idea. It would not only stop them from arguing but also it meant they wouldn't be so loud; in fact, they wouldn't be able to make any noise at all.

She went into the forest and cut down many strong vines. She then spliced them together, so she had just one, a mile long. She stretched out the vine, so the middle was in her garden and the rest disappeared into the bush on either side.

When they arrived later that day, she told them to walk in opposite directions, following the vine until they came to the end. A bird would fly above them. Then they must put the end of the vine in their mouths and make sure it was taught. When they were ready, the bird would fly back to Yopi, and when both birds had returned, she would beat a drum five times very loudly. On the fifth beat, both Bow and Cro must pull as hard as they could and the first one to pull the other to Yopi's garden would be the winner and be declared the strongest animal in the world.

All went well and on the fifth beat of the drum they started pulling, and sometimes Cro made ground and sometimes Bow made ground.

Since they had the vine in their mouths, they were unable to speak or make any other noise and it turned out that neither of them was really stronger than the other and so the battle continued. In fact, it still continues right up to this day.

So, if you are walking in the forest a few miles from Sugu in the province of Lae, be careful. Make sure You don't trip over a taut vine that is just above the ground.

August 1968

Chapter 1   Stella

This is ridiculous. I should feel great right now, on top of the world. Instead, I am as nervous as hell; my heart is pounding at thousands of beats per minute. Scared witless, basically.

I have just turned eighteen and find myself at a party in downtown Kuala Lumpur. It's a hot sticky night; the lights are dim and the music loud, and I am sitting next to probably the most beautiful girl in the world. Her name is Stella. She has long blonde hair and is wearing a blue T-shirt, a red miniskirt and her feet are bare. Unbelievably she has chosen to spend the evening with me ....

I shouldn't really be in Kuala Lumpur at all. By now, I should be in Madang, a town in Papua New Guinea. I had flown BOAC from Heathrow, my first time on a plane. I remember thinking about how I could make the sandwich that my mum had made for me, last the whole journey, and then suddenly, a lady in a smart blue uniform put a meal in front of me. I told her I didn't have any money to pay for it. She laughed and said it was a free gift from the airline. In fact, they kept giving me free food and drink. Everyone was so nice.

We stopped to refuel in Calcutta and had to leave the plane. We were told to be back in two hours. As I left the aircraft, I was almost knocked backwards by the heavy moist air that hit me.

Inside the terminal, the atmosphere was just as humid as outside, and the air had a sweet but bitter taste. People there were wearing beautiful clothes and seemed to talk at enormous speed without taking a breath, often shaking their heads from side to side as if they didn't agree with what they were saying themselves. There were also many beggars in rags and unbelievably undernourished. They looked exhausted and desperate. It occurred to me that I had seen very few non-white people or beggars in the flesh before.

On one side of the airport, there was a group of musicians and dancers. They wore loose clothing that shone like satin. They were so colourful in their vivid reds, greens and yellows. I was transfixed and watched until they stopped for a break. In fact, I was so mesmerised I forgot the time and only just got back to the plane before it took off.

The next stage of the journey would take us to Australia but as we flew over the Bay of Bengal, I realised there was a commotion at the front of the plane and several flight attendants had run up to deal with it. Soon afterwards, I saw one of them walking down the aisle, looking from side to side. When she reached me, she stopped, and I noticed that she had a bruise on her cheek.

"Hello, you're Richard Masters, aren't you?" I nodded. "Richard, I'm Tess. Are you with Voluntary Service Overseas on your way to Papua New Guinea?" I nodded again. "Do you have your malarial tablets handy?" I was getting pretty proficient at nodding. "Can I see them?" She looked at the bottle. "I won't be a minute."

She took the bottle, walked up the aisle, knocked on a door and went inside of what I thought must be the cockpit. A few minutes later, she returned, stooped down beside me and took my hand in both of hers.

"Richard, just now, we had a problem with a girl called Janet. She is also on VSO. She had been prescribed two malarial tablets a day instead of two per week and it turns out you have as well. Janet had a fit a few minutes ago and my colleague Angela and I had a real struggle to hold her down and stop her from hurting herself, as you can see," she pointed to her cheek. "The thing is, she is quite a small person and you are not and the pilot doesn't think it's safe to continue on to Australia. Anyway, we are going to land at Kuala Lumpur Airport, and you, Janet and her friend Carol will disembark there. I don't want you to worry, Richard; you will be looked after."

I felt as if she was treating me like a kid but the truth was that's exactly what I needed her to do. I felt upset and kind of lost.

So it was that, in an unscheduled stop in Kuala Lumpur, Janet, her friend Carol, and I (I didn't have a friend) were shown off the plane into the hands of the United Kingdom Diplomatic Service.

Janet and Carol were met by a young man and whisked away in the High Commissioner's staff car to be taken to his official residence.

A few minutes later, a tall, thin, middle-aged man, wearing a cream coloured suit and a red tie, introduced himself as Mr. Kelly. He had an Irish accent and told me he was a diplomat at the British High Commission and I would be staying with him until I could continue my journey. We were driven to his house in a very fine limousine, where I was introduced to his family.

"This is my wife, Mrs Kelly and my seven children, Beatrice, Camilla, Angus, Winston, Quentin, Leo and Maximilian. Maximilian is your age, and he has just finished school, Oxford for him in October. Anyway, he'll see you know the ropes and look after you."

"Pleased to meet you." I said, bowing slightly. I hadn't meant to bow and there was a bit of giggling from the boys. The truth is, when the family had been introduced, the image of Snow White and the Seven Dwarfs had come into my mind and I had struggled not to smile.

Mrs Kelly ran the house with the help of servants. I would guess she was in her forties and she was a very good looking woman. She was always very smartly dressed. Angus and Winston were young enough to live in Kuala Lumpur and the others were at various public schools in England. It was the summer holidays, and all were at home.

Of the five older Kellys, two were girls and kept themselves to themselves. The two oldest boys, Leo and Maximilian, were somewhat overbearing, and I was rather in awe of them and the confidence they exuded. I noticed that whenever they spoke to me their accent, which already sounded very public school to a boy from a working-class background, suddenly became posher still. They also had a habit of standing on either side and talking across me rather than to me directly. If it was designed to intimidate me, it worked. They managed to make me feel inferior at every turn and I had never experienced anything like it before. They made me feel very uncomfortable.

6

That afternoon, I had tea with them all. The tea was served by servants in white jackets. The room in which we sat was quite extraordinary. Looking back now, I am reminded of it when I visit the dining rooms of houses at National Trust properties. The lower part of the walls seemed to be made of a dark brown wood. I had never seen anything like that before. The ceiling was white and gold with small domes hanging down.

On the walls were huge, colourful paintings depicting bloodthirsty battle scenes and a smaller, framed photograph of the Queen. A chandelier dominated the room and was set over a very large table, of which we only took up half, even though there were a lot of us. It was covered with a beautiful lace tablecloth. As if I wasn't impressed enough, the cutlery was solid silver and the cups and plates looked so delicate that I feared that even if a fly landed on one of them, they would break into pieces.

I was asked a host of questions, and they politely pretended to listen to the answers, but the truth is my life story was not all that fascinating, that being an understatement. Really, I think they were teasing me. Perhaps it was a game to see who could get the most boring fact out of me. I could imagine them laughing about it later.

"Leo, when you asked him if he preferred Latin or Greek at school and he said he liked woodwork, that was a hoot."

"Yes, but you won, Max; with your question, who was his favourite group, and he said the Bee Gees. Can you believe it, the Bee Gees? Oh my, what a warthog!" (Leo had a habit of calling people animal names: donkey, warthog and wombat being his favourites)

The next day was difficult; I am not an extrovert, hopeless at small talk, especially with people I don't know, so I spent most of the day hanging around in my room as much as possible.

In the afternoon, I was asked, in a somewhat resentful tone, if I wanted to come to a party that evening. I had overheard a discussion earlier between Mrs Kelly and Maximilian.

"Mother, Leo and I are off to the Barrington-Stevenson's tonight. We'll need a lift."

"Of course, darling, but you'll have to take the boy with you."

"Which boy?"

"Oh, what's his name? Robert." (close)

"Do we really have to, Mummy?"

"Of course you do, darling. He's our guest."

"Oh, all right."

Later he came to find me.

"Roger (close), do you want to go to a party tonight? You don't have to if you don't want to."

Despite having limited clothing and nowhere to buy more, even if I had the money, I managed to make myself look for what passes as presentable in the Masters' household.

About forty youngsters were at the party; all knew each other, and some of their accents made the Kellys sound common. The girls sat and chatted or danced with each other, and the boys just made a lot of noise. I sat down and tried to look moody and magnificent as I had been schooled by my friend Pooh in an earlier life.

The last thing I expected was that I would have a good time, but incredible things happen when you least expect them.

8

When Stella came and sat next to me, I was pleased and uncomfortable in equal measures. I was not terribly knowledgeable about girls and the like. She was lovely; her voice was soft and kind, and she had a confident air. Although the lights were dim, I was sure she was unbelievably gorgeous. We talked and danced for hours.

I noticed that the boys and girls were mixing now; in fact, a crowbar wouldn't have prised them apart. Stella and I danced a lot, sometimes leaping wildly about and sometimes locked together, our innocent bodies pressing hard against each other. It was, without doubt, the best evening of my short life.

.... Now, we are sitting next to each other, we have run out of words and I feel I should make a move, perhaps kiss her, put a hand on her leg or offer to have sex with her or something, anything. I really don't know what to do, and my stomach is churning with worry and fear. One false move now, and I could lose my one true love forever.

I should explain; I lack confidence if you haven't already guessed. All my schools were boys only and I have never really had a girlfriend, in fact, I had never even kissed a girl in any meaningful way. I certainly don't know how to do sex.

Apparently, my oldest brother Gordon was sixteen when my mum persuaded my dad that he should tell Gordon the facts of life. So, he went into his bedroom one evening and nervously said,

"Son, I want to talk to you about sex."

Gordon replied, "yes Dad, what do you want to know?"

9

Dad stalked out of the room and never mentioned the subject again, to any of us. Thanks, Gordon!

I pluck up all my courage. "Shall we go somewhere quieter?" I say, on the brink of exploding. To my massive relief, she laughs and says.

"No, of course not; we've only just met. Anyway, my parents will be here any minute. Will you be at the club tomorrow?"

"Sure," I say. I have no idea where the club is, but I do know I'll be there unless, during the night, I'm kidnapped, tied up, gagged and buried deep in the ground.

"See you there then," she says, and kisses me on the lips for at least twenty seconds, and leaves. WOW! I surely know what heaven is.

That night I lay in bed, unable to sleep. Yesterday I had been in the depths of despair, and now I felt as high as a kite. Two days ago, I had been on my way to Papua New Guinea to teach for a year, and now I'm in love forever and will probably never leave Malaysia.

The club turns out to be the British Club, exclusively for the families of diplomats, business executives and the like. When Stella arrives, I am lying by the pool, trying to look cool with my genuine Millets jungle hat over my eyes. She kicks me gently in the ribs, and the hat falls off. I assume she does not like what she sees in the cold light of day. Basically, she takes no further interest in me from that moment on.

Later that afternoon, I wander over and sit next to her but I can find nothing to say. After an embarrassing few minutes, she gets up and walks away. Strangely, her attitude towards me is not as painful as I would have thought. I am disappointed, but now, I just want to get to New Guinea

In bed that night, my thoughts turned to just a few days earlier when I said goodbye to my parents and walked along that long straight passage at Heathrow towards the departure gate, feeling their presence behind me. I knew my mum was crying; she had put on such a brave face, encouraging me to go yet knowing we might never meet again. My mother had a heart problem; we both knew there was a possibility she could die while I was away. All I really wanted to do was turn round and run back, but I didn't.

The next day Janice and Carol arrive to take me on a tour of the city. They have been given a car for their use, a chauffeur to drive it and servants to attend to their every need; in fact, they have been given pretty well anything they wanted.

As we drive around Kuala Lumpur, it seems to me to be a lovely city, busy and relaxed, with many different nationalities represented on its dusty streets. There is an atmosphere of splendour about the place and many of the buildings are elegant and beautiful. At one point, I see a magnificent building and ask if it is the presidential palace. The driver tells me it is the railway station.

That evening one of the boys tells me there is a party that night. It doesn't come as a shock; there is a party every night. By day, the kids of the British Diplomatic Service lounge by the pool and play tennis. They have high tea with their mums and dads; as far as I could tell, that is the only contact they do have with them, and in the evening, they kiss, cuddle and fondle each other at parties until their parents drag them away.

The party turns out to be a very unpleasant and embarrassing affair, with Stella and I, trying to avoid each other. The Kelly kids, who obviously feel I have outstayed my welcome, spend the evening whipping up anti-state school education sentiments. I feel isolated and spend most of my evening sitting in the garden on my own.

At the end of the party, a mother enters the room to find her son lying on the floor with a girl, both wrapped in a Union Jack. He asks her to come back in a few minutes as he needs time to adjust himself somewhat. There is a great deal of laughter around the room, although the mum does not look terribly amused.

Altogether I have spent five days in Kuala Lumpur. I am grateful to the Kellys for putting me up, although I suspect they had no choice, but I am relieved that the time has come to leave.

I wonder if families like the Kellys still exist in the world's great capitals.

One hundred years ago, Kiku and Tifo were very important elders in the village of Tapoo in what is now called Madang province. They always had the final say whenever any important village decisions were being discussed. The problem was that they never agreed on anything and always opposed each other.

If Kiku said the Sing Sing should be on the next full moon, Tifo would insist it was to be held when the moon was new.

If Tifo wanted the new hut to be built at the east end of the village, Kiku would say that the only sensible place was to build it to the west of the village.

Everyone else was fed up with them as nothing ever got done, but they were very powerful, and there was nothing anybody could do.

One day Kiku told Tifo that he had found the perfect place to build a well for the village and that he would announce it at the next village gathering. He told Tifo where the well would be sited but asked him to keep it to himself till then.

At the time, the village women had to walk two miles to fetch water in their bamboos, so Tifo knew this would make Kiku very popular.

Tifo was in a difficult position. He would have to justify his reasons if he opposed such an important and popular proposal. The best way would be to find a better site. He decided to go and see where Kiku was suggesting.

Kiku had guessed that is what Tifo would do, but the spot he had suggested was surrounded by quicksand and very dangerous.

Tifo approached the place, not realising he was in danger, but before he could do anything, he was being sucked under. He struggled and fought but, in the end, he just disappeared. It was a dreadful way to die.

Kiku made sure that he was with plenty of other people at the time of Tifo's disappearance, so he could not be accused of having anything to do with it.

Kiko was now the village leader and could make all the decisions he wanted. He didn't really care if they were good for the village as long as they were good for him.

Tifo's older sister had magical powers. She was a Sanguma. However, she had never used her powers, and no one else knew. She was sure Kiku had murdered her brother and that he had died slowly, suffering terrible fear and pain. She decided to punish Kiku.

For the next year, every decision that Kiku made went disastrously wrong. He decided on the site for a new communal garden, but nothing would grow. He designed a new meeting house and ordered the men of the village to build it. The night after it was completed, it fell to pieces, injuring several people, including one of the elders.

To try to regain the respect of the people, he announced a Sing Sing and said he would provide four of his best pigs for the feast. When the meal was served, the pork was a green colour and everyone who ate it became sick. The Sing Sing had to be cancelled.

It was the last straw. One night, the villagers went to his house, put his belongings in a sack and took him to the edge of the village. They told him they would kill him if he ever returned to the village.

Today, people who live in or are visiting Tapoo occasionally catch a glimpse of an old man with a sack over his shoulder, wandering through the bush near the village, hoping to be allowed back in.

Chapter 2   The Boat

Having reached Darwin, we boarded another aeroplane which took us to Port Moresby, the capital of New Guinea, and then a third to Madang. Each plane was half the size of the one before. I was looking forward to seeing some of Papua New Guinea from the air, but it was dark by the time we took off. We occasionally saw lights below us, but even those were rare.

We were staying about twenty miles from Madang in Alexishafen, the headquarters of the catholic mission.

Madang is a coastal town and is the capital of Madang Province. We were driven there the following day. Its centre had stores mainly run by Chinese or Australians, some European shops and a few dainty tea rooms. There was also a cinema, various businesses and several churches. Surrounding all these were pleasant, quiet streets with houses mainly occupied by white people.

Further out still were areas of housing where native New Guineans tended to live. The houses were made of wood, foliage, and sometimes, corrugated iron for the roofs. Close by were gardens for growing vegetables and keeping chickens, and beyond was the start of the forest and bush. The sea lay to the south.

It was a strange place, unusual and exciting. People were poor in terms of money, but there was no shortage of food or clean water, so life could have been worse.

The indigenous people who lived there came from all over the province. They wore ragged European clothing and were poorly paid. Some couldn't find work at all. I spoke to a few who had learnt English and they told me they would have liked to go home, but their families pressured them to stay and send money back to the village so they could buy goods from mission stores. In the villages of New Guinea, working to earn money was rare.

The other volunteers had been in Madang for over a week and were getting bored; there was little to do in the mission or in town.

A girl called Heather told me how she had gone to the cinema with a group of other people. It was a Roy Rogers cowboy movie, and the small picture house was packed. Suddenly, in the middle of the film, a man stood on his seat and shouted that he was Roy Rogers and those from other places were like the baddie scum. Many others jumped up, and much verbal abuse was given and taken. It was not long before they started fighting, and as the girls ran for it, a pitched battle was taking place.

Someday I will write to the producers of Roy Rogers to tell them of the mayhem their gentle movies were causing.

The following day, we were called together to be told our final destinations. We were to depart the morning after. The Bishop of Madang was there to bless us. We were all being sent to Catholic Divine Word Missions, although many of us, including me, were Church of England or non-religious.

About twenty volunteers and as many again priests and brothers were squeezed into the small room. It was baking hot and I was already sweating, even at nine in the morning. Father John was responsible for volunteers and their placements. He stepped forward and raised his hand for quiet. He started reading the list.

"Sarah Kiernan, you are going to Catholic Mission Boret, a beautiful coastal place with golden beaches, azure seas and palm trees. The people in the nearby villages are very friendly, and many of them have turned to Christianity. It has purpose built classrooms and a very modern medical centre; it is a thriving community."

They were read out one after the other, and each one seemed like a paradise on earth to me. As each was called, the priests and brothers clapped their hands with joy and hugged the volunteer and the bishop blessed the lucky recipient.

Just three of us were left now and I detected a change in the atmosphere. All those in the know seemed to straighten and look solemn and knowledgeable; something special was coming; I could feel it.

"For the first time, we are sending volunteers into the interior of the country and the challenges here will be very different. You three have been selected."

There was warm applause and much nodding of heads. The names of the other two were read out, and I heard a number of encouraging remarks.

"Richard Masters, you are going to Catholic Mission Giri, run by Father Miozga."

Not a sound; the silence was absolutely deafening, and it may have been my imagination, but my blessing seemed longer than all the others.

At the end of the gathering, everybody rushed over to the map on the wall where all the different mission stations were marked; the excitement was tangible. After some time, the last few filed out. I walked over to the map and found Catholic Mission Giri. It was a long way inland, but there was a road. It ran from a small town on the coast called Bogia. Some way north of Bogia, a vast river flowed into the sea. The River Ramu came from the mountains further South and east and, at one point, seemed to be only a few miles from Giri. I wondered if I was flying to Bogia.

The following day, there was a delay, and we actually left late afternoon, and, as it turned out, we were going by boat.

When I look back over all my years, there is only one memory that still brings dryness to my throat and sweat to my brow; it was that boat journey. It lasted sixteen hours and seemed like eternal hell. No wonder we had been blessed before we left.

There were six volunteers on the boat, which was a copra carrier. It had the look of a miniature tug. There was a small cabin behind the wheelhouse and a forward deck where the volunteers gathered. There was a large cargo area below for copra and other goods, but for our journey, it was empty. That meant the boat was very high in the water. I did not know then, but empty copra boats were incredibly unstable and bob around alarmingly in rough seas.

The Flame of Madang had a crew of three, all reassuringly laid back and not so reassuringly downing rum as if there was no tomorrow. It was a beautiful warm day with a cool breeze and a calm sea. We all lay

19

down on the forward deck and prepared to relax. Jane, who was to be the first to disembark, told me she lived in East Anglia and regularly sailed on the Norfolk Broads; she was really looking forward to this part of the journey.

The skipper, who was dressed a bit like a pirate who had lost his parrot, laughed and sent the mate to talk to us.

"Yupella i come quick bec," he said in faltering English, "yu drown you cam back; se i bicpella tru."
This, I learnt later, means the sea is very rough.

We all looked around and could see nothing untoward and ignored the advice. I leant over the rail and wondered what all the fuss was about.

A few minutes later, the boat left the protection of Madang Harbour and the first massive wave hit us. I felt it crash into me, pinning me to the railing. The boat then seemed to dip and dive and then slowly straighten. I was winded, and when I came round, I realised the bag I had been holding, which contained my camera, address book, change of clothes and the food for the journey, had gone and I was soaked. I tried to shout to the captain that my things had gone overboard, but at that moment, the next wave smashed into me. The boat lent over so far that the deck was actually in the sea and then bobbled back and leaned as far the other way. I was violently sick. It was awful.

Wave after wave hit us; it went on for hour after hour. I was clinging onto the railing, constantly vomiting, staring at the shore, a mile away, and working out all the time where I could swim to when the boat eventually and inevitably capsized. I was not a strong swimmer and knew in my heart that there would be no chance of surviving; I would drown in a few minutes. I was soaked, shivering with cold and very frightened.

Night came with no relief; it just made me more aware of the stink of petrol fumes and the stench of rotting coconut meat. I was vaguely aware of the others suffering around me, but none of us was able to offer help to anyone else.

Sometime during the night, I decided to give up the fight, let go of the rail and let death be my relief; I had long since emptied my stomach, and every bout of retching brought acute pain. Exhausted, I slid to the floor and put my head between my knees. I cannot imagine why, but Sunday lunches from ten or so years ago came into my mind when my brother Colin was still at home. Mum always thickened the cream to go with the apple crumble and would give us a whisk each to lick. Colin would bring me mine, look me in the eye and give it a slow, elaborate lick before handing it over with a smirk. I used to spend the rest of the day thinking up elaborate ways I could torture him to pay him back. The memory gradually faded.

I heard a voice, but was I in heaven or hell? Was it an Angel or the devil himself?

"Young man, wake up; you can come ashore. You are at Catholic Mission Barbara."

Heaven, I guessed.

I looked up and realised the sun was up; it was morning. A kindly looking priest was standing over me offering me his hand. We had docked and everything was calm; the others were being helped ashore.

The priest and his staff were obviously very used to the victims of the copra boats. Once on land, they encouraged us to change our clothes, sip cool green coconut milk, lie on the warm beach and sleep. We all did exactly that, although I had to borrow some clothes from the mission.

We were all young and strong, both mentally and physically; otherwise, we would not have been chosen to come.

When we woke up, it was midday. We felt much better and we were all hungry. We ate our fill and, minus Jane were put back on the boat. I was annoyed as I had missed the opportunity to ask Jane if the boat trip had met her expectations!

One by one, the others were dropped off. Each placement was exactly as it had been described: a tropical paradise. I wondered, not for the first time, what the interior would be like.

I was devastated at losing my bag, particularly the camera with many photos of the flight, Calcutta and Kuala Lumpur. I had learnt a lesson that was to repeat itself over and over again; the crew could have told me to put my bag somewhere safe when I boarded. I suppose I was brought up expecting people to look after my welfare. Here, they didn't, not because they were malicious but because they assumed you knew. In New Guinea, it never occurred to anyone that you were new and lacked experience. You learned the hard way.

By the afternoon, I was the only one left. I lay on my back on the deck, staring contentedly at nothing in particular, listening to the mate telling me I should come on the boat when there's a real storm, then I would see some excitement.

Finally, Bogia came into sight.

I had it in my mind that it would be a busy port with lots of ships and activity. It turned out to be nothing of the sort; it had a small docking pier and was the main and only town in Bogia district. To call it a town was something of an exaggeration; as far as I could tell, it was just a mission station with a very fine church, a cattle ranch and a general store.

I hoped I would be able to sleep that night. I was nervous and excited in equal measures; tomorrow, with a bit of luck, I would be sleeping in my new home in Catholic Mission Giri.

The following day I was standing outside the door of the mission talking to Father William, the priest of the Bogia mission, when a Jeep roared around the corner at enormous speed and skidded to a halt in front of me. A huge bear of a man jumped out, gave me a ferocious hug and introduced himself.

"Hello Richard, I am Brother Vasavious from Mikarew, about three-quarters of the way to Giri. Get in, get in."

I said goodbye to the priest. He bade me a safe journey and laughed as he wished me well in the sago swamps. I didn't know what he meant, but it certainly sounded ominous.

Once in the jeep, Vasavious patted me hard on the shoulder.

"I am what people call a hearty German who never stops talking," he roared with laughter; I laughed with him. It was impossible not to.

He entertained me with stories of Germany and New Guinea as he drove the old jeep over a road that in

23

England would have been a very rough track or even a footpath in places.

Occasionally, we would pass someone walking and Vasavious would always stop, get out of the jeep and chat for a few minutes in Pidgin English. Sometimes he gave them a lift for a few miles. I had no idea what was being said but they always seemed pleased to see him.

It was a great few hours, listening to the brother and watching the forests, grasslands and rivers pass by. I asked if there was any jungle. He answered,

"Yes, yes, plenty of jungle in New Guinea," but then plenty of this or plenty of that was his stock answer to most questions. I liked Vasavious; he seemed honest and friendly, and he made the area sound colourful and exciting. However, he would answer no questions about Giri; all he would say was.

"Wait and see."

We screeched to a halt in a cloud of dust and insects, and in front of me was a house that was part of the mission station of Brother Vasavious. It was huge, maybe sixty feet long and forty feet wide. It was built on stilts and was made of wood and some kind of large leaves for the roof. Two people sat on the veranda drinking beer from the bottle. One of them, Father Fritz, came down to greet me. He could speak no English, but it was evident that he did not need to. Brother Vasavious was his mouth and ears. I was led onto the balcony and given a beer.

"This," announced Vasavious grandly, "is Father George Miozga, the Fuhrer of Giri."

Being called that obviously annoyed him and he gazed at Vasavious without a hint of a smile. We shook hands; he had a firm grip and his eyes never left mine. They were watery blue, intense and quite frightening. I looked away first, and the atmosphere lightened somewhat. He nodded slightly, as if he had won some sort of first encounter. During the next half hour, Vasavious chatted on, with occasional input from myself and Father Fritz. George Miozga said nothing.

We rose to leave, and as we walked towards the vehicle, I asked the father what he would like me to call him.

"Father George." He replied.

He didn't ask, so I told him I wanted to be called Richard; it was better than Dick, the name I had ended up with in England.

As we walked towards our vehicle, I was slightly behind Father George and was able to look at him properly for the first time. He was not a tall man but looked trim and powerful. His head seemed too big for his body and he wore glasses with small round lenses.

He introduced me to his vehicle, the Unimog.

Now you will not find the Unimog in the showrooms of England nor on the cover of Auto Car. To me, it looked like a tank but with the gun turret removed and replaced with a winch with thick, strong cable. It was large, overbearing and about the only four-wheeled vehicle that could make it to Giri.

I soon realised that the road was atrocious and made the previous one seem like a motorway. The noise of the engine and the constant crashing as we hit huge bumps followed by deep craters made it impossible to talk. I was uncomfortable but soon found that the trick to making it bearable was to relax and let my body become, sort of, floppy. Anyway, I didn't care; after the boat, this was luxury.

We passed through dense forest, tall grassed areas, swamps and by a few houses where people ran out to wave to us. I waved back but the father ignored them. We drove over raging torrents and through fast flowing streams; no concrete bridges here, just rows of rough logs laid across from one side to the other. Twice, the vehicle failed to negotiate a steep incline and had to be winched up.

"Watch how it is done," said Father George, "you will have to do this yourself."

This alarmed me somewhat. I told him that I had only just passed my driving test a few months ago and did not feel very confident. If he heard, he gave no indication, something I was to get very used to.

We arrived at night, and I had no real first impressions of Giri. I was taken into a small hut on stilts and shown a bed buried below a heavy mosquito net.

I lay in bed listening to the sounds of the night, frogs croaking, insects clicking and the birds shrieking. I wondered what my first day would be like and how I should approach it. I felt very excited but also a little concerned in case I messed up and couldn't cope.

Unable to sleep, I thought about what had led me to apply for VSO.

I started my secondary education at Goldsworth School for Boys in Woking and, on inexplicably passing the thirteen plus, was transferred to George Abbot School for Boys near Guildford. By some miracle, they got me nine O-level passes, all with low grades, but I didn't care. I was astounded and I think my mum and dad were also pretty amazed but also really pleased.

I studied for three A-levels, and it took me about a week to realise I was totally out of my depth. The truth was, I just wasn't clever enough.

I enjoyed my geology lessons enormously; they gave me a lifelong love for the subject, but maths and physics were just a mystery.

Big Boy Thomas and I were the only sixth formers not to have been chosen to be sub-prefects or prefects. Big Boy Thomas was pretty odious, although, oddly, he wasn't that big. Why I wasn't chosen, I couldn't imagine. All this was to change the day I saw the VSO poster.

I do not really look back on my school days with happy memories. I was not a popular person and nor was I particularly good at anything. I lived miles away from the school, so I kind of missed out on friends in school and at home. I saw VSO as a possibility for a fresh start and sent for an application form. I had to put down two referees, of which one had to be my headteacher; that was bad news. My second would be my venture scout leader, Rod 'Rabbit' Taylor (he always claimed he bred at the same rate as a rabbit, although I never saw any evidence of that). We got along really well; I'd be all right there. I was not much good academically or at sports, but I had been in the cubs, scouts and venture scouts and loved the physical outdoor activities. As it happened, my headteacher was a great supporter of VSO and was often invited to be part of one of their interview panels. He had never had a pupil apply before. The outcome was that I was

27

promoted to full prefect in seconds and got an excellent reference.

Sleep finally came.

The Copra Boat   Painted by Val Naden

Different seasons but one thing in common. They all show parts of the road from Mikarew to Giri

Road leading to the church in Bogia

Unimog is winched up a slippery slope

The first cassowary was once the same size as a Wren. He was a greedy bird and stole food from all the other birds.

The melampitta was enjoying a meal of insects when suddenly the cassowary swooped down, stole all of them and gobbled them down.

The following day, the crowned pigeon was just about to eat his tea of snails when, out of nowhere, the cassowary grabbed them and flew away, swallowing them down whole as he went.

The next day, the honey eater was enjoying some sweet nectar when down came the cassowary, tearing the whole plant from the ground and eating everything.

The bird of paradise thought she was safe from the greedy cassowary. She was at the very top of the tallest tree in the forest and had collected some excellent fruit for her supper. Just as she was about to eat, the cassowary crashed into the branch she was sitting on and the fruit fell to the ground. Before the bird of paradise had time to move, the cassowary had flown down and eaten all the fruit.

One sunny afternoon, the cassowary noticed a bird up in a tree eating some grubs.

'Umm,' he thought, 'they look delicious. 'I will steal them; they will make a very tasty snack.'

He flapped his wings, but to his surprise, nothing happened. He tried again and this time pushed with his feet as well but to no avail. Again and again he tried but he could not fly.

"Help, help." He tweeted loudly.

The melampitta and the crowned pigeon and the honeyeater and the bird of paradise all flew down to see what was going on. The cassowary cried out,

"Why can't I fly?"

The birds told him.

"You are so greedy you have become too fat and too big to fly, and you will never fly again."

They all laughed and flew around him, taunting him. He was very sad, not to mention hungry.

And that is why the cassowary can't fly.

Chapter 3   The Headteacher

The following morning, I met the teachers I was to work with. They were all native New Guineans, although none were local. They looked at me rather suspiciously; none of them had ever worked with a foreign colleague before. Father George introduced us and followed up with the bombshell.

"This is Master Richard Master." He paused and I think he felt he had made a joke and we would all laugh. Nobody did. I don't think he ever tried to be humorous again, not with me, anyway.

"These are our teachers: Peter, John, Ignatius, Johan and Philip." I shook hands with each. "Now, as you know, our school year runs from January to December, so there is no class for Richard to teach until after Christmas. He will, therefore, act as headteacher for this term. I will decide, at some stage, whether to employ an outsider to take over next term or allow him to continue."

Approaching Catholic Mission Giri from the northwest, a track from Mikarew passes through the village of Giri number 1 and climbs a gentle sandy palm tree-lined incline into the mission station. It is a large flat area at the top of a low hill, falling away steeply on either side into a mixture of bush and forest. On the far side, the track meanders its way southeast for a few miles to the village of Giri Number 2 and eventually to the mighty Ramu River. Just outside the mission, the first few hundred yards of the track are surrounded by coconut palms laid out in tidy rows. This is the copra plantation belonging to the mission.

All the buildings are made from rough wood from trees in the bush, coconut leaf thatch and the living quarters are on wooden stilts.

The mission has four main parts with a large church dominating the centre. Outside the church is an area of grass with two posts at either end. A group of three school buildings is to the South and the living quarters of the father and teachers to the north. There are boarding shacks for the pupils to the west and the mission shop and generator shed to the east.

The classrooms are two to each building with low thatch walls and no windows; they are cool and pleasant. In between each of the double classrooms is a small office. These are hot, airless affairs as the walls are built to the roof and there are no windows.

It was to one of these offices that I strode, a man of destiny, born to bypass all training and experience, a natural headteacher of style and brilliance, sent by some mighty power to help the natives. I found my office dirty and full of files crammed with old papers that appeared to have no significance. There was not even a space for me to sit down, let alone work. A good clear out was in order. I took the files out and burned them. I tidied the room, swept it out and sat savouring my handiwork.

I sat at my desk in my clean, tidy office and realised I had nothing to do, or, at least, no idea what I was supposed to do. After a while, I went outside and lit a cigarette. I saw Father George walking towards me.

"Richard, there is a young couple in Giri who want to get married in church. That is rare, but I need to check the girl's age before I agree. I will say yes if she is fifteen, but they will have to wait if she is younger," he looked into the office. "What have you done with all the records?"

A horrible burning sensation started in the pit of my stomach.

"I think I might have burnt them." I stuttered.

At first, he thought I was kidding and smiled, then he looked at my face and realised the awful truth. He let out a ferocious scream which seemed to last minutes. The other teachers ran out of their huts to see what on earth was happening. I thought for a second, he was going to physically attack me, and to be honest, at that moment, I would have preferred that to what happened next.

Father George was furious; no, he was beyond furious; he could not find the words or actions to express his rage. He shouted and ranted and humiliated me in front of the whole staff. I had never suffered such verbal abuse before in my short, protected life and had no defence or method of coping. The other teachers looked at the ground, and I think they felt sorry for me. On the other hand, they knew I had been stupid and there was no excuse.

What I had actually done was destroy history. I had burned the parish records since the mission had been set up forty years earlier, all the medical and birth records of the local people and valuable notes left by explorers, doctors, missionaries and gold prospectors over the years.

The following day, I felt hot and feverish and couldn't get up. I should have been present at the assembly when the Union Jack was raised and the national anthem was sung. I expect Father George would have introduced his new headteacher to the pupils.

The following two months were awful. Apathy took complete hold of me; there was nothing for me to do anyway. I was continually plagued with a fever, real or psychological. I got up late and had no work to do. I put on weight and made no attempt to get to know or make contact with the people in local villages. I also found the heat between mid-morning and the late afternoon rains unbearable, and the skin on my legs and back itched continually.

To make matters worse, I broke the generator, the only source of electricity. It provided light to all the classrooms and some of the mission houses. (The villages had no source of power of any kind) It was the usual story; the first time I was asked to start it, I protested that I didn't even know what a generator looked like. Vague instructions were given to me, but basically, I was expected to be able to do these things. I was told to stop whinging and get on with it. It took the father two days to fix it.

To me, it seemed he had nothing but contempt for me, and to be honest, I felt the same about myself. I now realise that I was suffering from depression. It manifested itself in many ways; it often felt as though my chest was being crushed, and sometimes, even breathing was difficult. I would start to cry for no apparent reason. I felt homesick, lonely and lacked any purpose. I desperately needed help but didn't know how to get it; there was no one I could ask. Apart from meals and occasional walks around the school area, I spent my whole time in my room. I avoided other people as much as possible.

We had no form of communication with the outside world apart from letters. These took anything from two to four weeks to get home and the same to come back from England. I knew it would worry them, but I eventually wrote to my mum and dad, and although I didn't tell them the whole story, I indicated I was unhappy and was thinking of coming home.

In November, the bishop responsible for all education in Madang Province visited. He asked to speak to me, noting my late arrival at the breakfast table and listened carefully as I expounded my ridiculous views to him. I guess telling a roman catholic bishop that there is far too much religion taught in the curriculum is a little naive to say the least, but it did not occur to me at the time, nor did I really care.

A few weeks later, Father George showed me a letter ordering me to pack my bags and return to Madang from where I would be placed in a mission where I could be appropriately supervised.

I was really surprised by the father's reaction. I thought he would be pleased to have an opportunity to get rid of me. Since my arrival, he had shown me no affection whatsoever; his attitude was one of disdain. The letter infuriated him, however. He asked me to think about it and tell him the following morning whether I wanted to stay or go.

That night, I thought back to the first hurdle I encountered when I applied to be accepted for VSO.

I received a letter telling me I had been granted an interview and was to report to VSO headquarters in

Hanover Square. Ten days later, I travelled up to London from Woking on the early morning train.

The interview panel comprised of a headmistress, a retired naval officer and a doctor. They were stern but kind and asked the sort of questions you would expect; why do you want to go? I want excitement and to help others. Where? An out of the way place where I could do the most good, and so on. I thought at the time that I'd done OK and celebrated with lunch at Joe Lyons in the strand and a look around Stanley Gibbons stamp shop before getting the train home.

A week later, I received a letter; I had made it through to the next round of my application. I remember feeling elated and excited.

I couldn't help myself; I started to cry at the memory.

In my mind, I went through a hundred reasons why I should leave. I couldn't think of a single one to make me stay. I was desperate to get away. The problem was, I knew with absolute certainty that I couldn't leave. Somewhere, deep down, there was a voice saying, 'If you leave now, you will regret it for the rest of your life.'

I imagined standing in front of my Mum, Dad, Colin, Pooh, my Headteacher and saying.

"I had to leave. I was lonely. I didn't feel very well. The nasty man was mean to me."

The following morning, I did something that, in hindsight, I think was one of the bravest and best decisions I have ever made; I told Father George I would like to stay. He tore up the letter and wrote a stinker back, refusing to let me go. I have no idea why he did this; perhaps poor company was better than no company in his mind.

A few weeks later, the term ended, and I was relieved of my post as headteacher and told I would have my own class in January; I knew that the person who would replace me would be arriving shortly. Life was about to change dramatically.

I was surprised to receive a letter from my dad; he was not a letter writer and always left that sort of thing to my mum. It was short and to the point.

'Son, I'm so sorry you're having a bad time. If you want to come home, that's absolutely fine, but I think you'll regret it if you do. The thing is; however bad things are, they will always get better, always. Mum sends her love and will write soon. Keep well. Lots of love, Dad.'

Wise man, my dad.

In the village of Attangra, in the foothills of the Highlands, lived a man and his wife. He was a cruel man and treated his wife badly, he insulted her in public and called her names; sometimes, he didn't let her eat for days and did not allow her to have friends or see her family.

All these things he was allowed to do under village tradition and law. However, he could not beat her, that was taboo. As her father was a powerful village elder, he did not dare break that rule.

Every year she had a baby, and because her husband could see how much pleasure she got from the child, he was jealous and angry and would give the baby to other families in exchange for betelnuts and salt.

When she had the fifth baby, a boy, she could not bear to lose him. The day before he was due to go to another family, she ran away with him, deep into the bush. She made a shelter and foraged for food, and for the first time in many years, she was happy.

Her husband was very angry, and every day he went into the bush and searched for her, but he could find no sign of her. Then, one day, he had an idea. He had three dogs that he kept in his house. One was large and aggressive. He got some clothes that belonged to his wife and made the dog sniff the clothes. At the same time, he beat the dog. He then tied a rope around the dog's neck and took him into the bush, hoping the dog would pick up the scent of his wife.

Unbeknown to him, he was always followed by one of his wife's brothers on their father's orders, as he suspected he might have killed her and hidden her body or be keeping her prisoner somewhere.

On the third day, the dog picked up the wife's scent. The dog became very excited. It pulled so hard the husband could not keep hold of the rope and the dog escaped and ran to where the woman was.

When it found her, she was up a tree picking fruit. Her baby was lying on the floor. The dog attacked the baby, tossed him in the air and then shook him until he died.

When she had scrambled down the tree, she ran to her baby and found that he was dead. She grabbed a sharpened stick and speared and killed the dog.

When the husband arrived, he was so angry that he lost control and hit his wife with a rock.

Her brother was a very powerful man. When he saw what had happened, he got hold of the husband and knocked him to the ground. He tied him up and took him back to the village. He told his Father that the husband had hit his daughter with a rock, and he had seen it happen.

This is what their father had been waiting for; the taboo had been broken. He ordered the man to be tied to a tree and the family took turns beating him with sticks. The man begged them to stop, but they ignored him and beat him even harder. Finally, a noose was placed around the husband's neck, and he was hanged from a branch and died.

All the women in the village went to find the wife to console her and tell her she was safe, that her husband was dead. But when they found her, she was weeping over her dead baby, and she was crying so much that a small rivulet of water had formed.

It was such an upsetting scene that all the women cried, and their tears flowed into the rivulet, and the rivulet became a stream and then a river. They called the river Ramu because that was the name of the dead little boy.

The women tried to make their friend return to the village with them, but she refused, and they left her crying over the dead baby.

The legend is that she is still crying, and while her tears flow, the mighty Ramu River will also flow, all the way to the sea.

Chapter 4   Giri Life

Over three hundred languages are still spoken in New Guinea, and years before, the Australians introduced Pidgin English (tok pisin) as a language to unify the country. Until then, I had unsuccessfully tried to learn it as a poor version of English. Now I was determined to master it properly. My teachers were the mission workers Bonnie and Hans. (I did suggest to Hans that he change his name to Clyde. Of course, he had no idea what I was talking about and looked somewhat confused)

Bonnie was an old man whose only possessions were a pair of shorts, a T-shirt and a mangy dog called Manham. Bonnie had ringworm; he loved life, his work and his dog. I adored Bonnie and spent many hours listening to his ramblings. Some of the stories in this book were told to me by him. Only once did I see him when he wasn't smiling.

Hans was tall, thin, young and ambitious. Several times, he had run off to seek his fortune. He always returned and because the father liked him, he took him back each time. Neither Bonnie nor Hans spoke any English.

After a month of serious study, I could speak tok pisin pretty much fluently. It helped to have a copy of the bible written entirely in Pidgin, called nupela testament, as well as one in English. I could compare the two.

It is a lovely language, and I still enjoy using it, particularly when reprimanding errant pupils.

"Yu long long pukpuk buskanaka!" (you foolish crocodile that comes from the bush; a serious insult in Giri)

Bonnie tested my language skills by telling me a story in tok pisin about his father, who had been a leader of his people in a village many miles upstream on the Ramu River. A fierce argument had broken out between his village and another a few miles away. War was inevitable, and it was left to people who had connections in both camps to arrange the time and place.

So, at dawn one morning, on a field of short kunai grass, the two armies faced each other, standing in lines about fifty or so yards apart.

There were over one hundred warriors on each side, and each was carrying three or four throwing spears. They were dressed for battle, naked apart from grass skirts, necklaces with animal teeth attached and headdresses with colourful feathers. The more important fighters had bird of paradise feathers, and all had red, white and black markings on their face and bodies.

Behind the warriors, the women started fires for cooking and the children played merrily; there was a carnival atmosphere.

At the appointed hour, the battle began. The warriors hurled their spears across the divide at their opposite number. They rarely hit anyone, as the lines of warriors were too far apart for that to happen. When they ran out of spears, they would dart forward and collect those that had been thrown at them. Occasionally, someone would be grazed doing this but there were no serious injuries.

The battle was regularly interrupted for meal breaks, and at sundown, it was declared over. Both groups then retired to their villages to celebrate victory, an event that often lasted several days and involved a great deal of eating and dancing.

Bonnie and I agreed it was a very sensible way to fight a war. More importantly, I understood everything and passed the language test.

Each week, I would spend two or three evenings with Father George. He seemed happy with this and I soon realised that he spent every evening alone before I arrived. He did not seem to have made any attempt to make friends with the Giri people.

Sometimes we played chess. He was very good and I don't think I ever won. Otherwise, he talked incessantly. He was a strange man, seemingly incapable of showing affection for anything that wasn't an inanimate object he could tinker with. Perhaps the reason was in his past.

He told me about his life in Poland. Like many Catholics, he had been persecuted, and his childhood had been incredibly hard, with everything being a struggle. Priesthood and, ultimately, missionary work had been an escape for him. He dreaded the inevitable day when he would be sent back.

He was a small man physically, but in the parish of Giri, he called the shots.

Some evenings, I would wander down to Giri number 1, the nearest settlement only a few minutes away.

A path ran to, and through the village and there were about twenty houses on either side. They were built from readily available materials: trees from the forest for the stilts and the main structure, bamboo for the flooring, palm leaves, straw, kunai grass and anything suitable for the walls and roof. The classrooms were made of the same materials.

Inside, there was just one room in which the extended family would live. The structure was usually twelve to twenty yards long and five to eight yards wide.   There was only one door which opened to a veranda where the family would sit to talk and exchange words with anyone passing.

The stilts protected the house from flooding but also from domestic and wild animals getting in and stealing food.

In front of each would be a patch of ground where their cooking fire would be cited. They would sit around the fire and eat their meal when the weather was good. This was a very social occasion as everybody could see each other's fire and would wander over to chat while they were eating.

Many households had dogs and some had pigs that scavenged around the houses; in fact, the more pigs you had, the higher your status in the village. I had never seen pigs like these; they were very much my idea of what a wild boar looks like. However, their size and temperament were quite different, as I was to find out later.

These pigs were only killed and eaten for special occasions, mainly for dances and festivals that took place every so often called Sing Sing.

Many people were related; Father George reckoned that of the two to three hundred people who lived in and around Giri Number 1, there were only five or six different families.

I would sit with the family around their fire and share stories or a meal with them. The staple foods were sago, yams, sweet potatoes and leaf vegetables. Occasionally, the men of the villages went hunting for larger game: wild boar and cassowary. However, these were hard to find, so they also ate rodents, grubs and pretty much anything they could catch.

One of the first times I had wandered through the village, I passed a young man sitting by his cooking fire. We nodded to each other, and on the way back, he stood and invited me to sit with him. He introduced himself as Joseph. I told him he should call me Richard. He called his wife and children down from the house and told me her name was Abi and the kids were Peter and Ruth. I shook hands with each of them. Abi kept her eyes averted and looked embarrassed. The only clothing she had on was a dark looking grass skirt. I had seen women dressed in this way at a distance but not close up and I had never seen a woman's breasts before coming to New Guinea; the women of Woking tended to wear tops in public. I think I looked at Abi for a moment too long.

Joseph grinned, "Nais tumas, eh?" (beautiful, eh?) I went red in the face and started to apologise. He laughed and slapped me on the back. He was right though; she was incredibly beautiful.

We all sat around the fire. Joseph, Peter and Ruth were quite vocal but Abi said very little.

I became particularly attached to Joseph and his family, and, as time went by, Abi opened up and lost much of her reserve. Joseph was a young man in his mid twenties, he thought he was twenty five, but could not be sure, and as someone had destroyed the parish records, he would probably never find out. He had married when he was sixteen and Abi was perhaps fifteen.

He was desperate to learn English as he intended, at some stage, to leave the village and get a good job in Madang. I started teaching him English and after a while Abi joined in, and in return, they taught me the basics of the very complicated local Giri language and any advanced Pidgin that had evaded me.

Sometime later, an Australian doctor visited. He had worked in the Lower and Middle Ramu for over thirty years. His hobby was learning the local languages of villages he visited, and he told me that he was fairly certain that we were the only two people from outside who could speak Giri fluently. I think he was being kind. My knowledge was rudimentary at best!

The evenings in the village would be spent listening to stories of New Guinea folklore, or sometimes, I would describe something from home in England, but mostly, we just got up to date with the gossip. One evening, Joseph surprised me by asking me if I would like him and Abi to be my New Guinean father and mother; they would like to adopt me. It sounded crazy, but then much of my life felt that way.

I talked to Father George, who thought the whole thing was daft but did not actually say no. So, I gained a second set of parents even though neither of them was more than a few years older than me.

I told them that I would be honoured to be their son, and we celebrated with a special meal that Abi prepared, comprising of small pieces of meat with yams cooked in coconut milk; it was very tasty. We chatted for a while and when I got up to leave, I asked Abi what the meat was.

"Rat," she said.

I managed to keep it together until I was out of sight and then I was violently sick. I decided in future, when presented with food I didn't recognise, I wouldn't wait until I'd eaten before asking what it was. Or better still, I wouldn't ask at all.

Those trips to Giri to chat and swap stories with Joseph and the other villagers were a highlight for me. Other evenings were spent playing chess with the father, writing letters or working in my room.

A few days after the rat culinary experience I decided to walk to Giri Number 2, which was a bit over two miles away. It was a hot, sultry morning and it wasn't long before I began to get tired.   I was also short of breath and found myself stopping at every stream to drink and rest. By the time I got there, the energy had been sucked out of my body and I was exhausted. I remember thinking to myself that in future, Giri Number 1 was going to be the limit of my walking exploits.

It was not to be, however. On arrival, I found myself surrounded by some of my pupils and other young villagers, excited that I had come to visit. They sat me down and gave me cool green coconut milk to drink. After a minute or two, a village elder and his son arrived to greet me formerly. He did not speak Pidgin English, so his son interpreted. We talked for a while and then he asked me what I thought about their river. He looked shocked when I said I hadn't seen it. He had an animated conversation with his son, whose name was Rabul.

"Come I will take you," he said, "it is not far."

"Thank you," I replied, my heart sinking and my mind desperately trying to think of an excuse not to go and failing miserably.

So, we set off, Rabul and I at the front and ten or so children and adults behind. The path was obviously well used and I wondered if they fished or perhaps it was their water source, I was too breathless to ask Rabul, as he set a stinging pace. I think it was further than my original journey to Giri Number 2, but I bravely pretended all was fine.

However, when I stepped out of the forest onto the bank of the river, all thoughts of fatigue left me. I was mesmerised. Rabul signalled the others to stay back and led me to within ten feet of the water.

The Ramu River was wide and fast flowing, not as wide as the Thames that I had seen in London a number of times but wide, nevertheless. There was a great deal of detritus floating by, mainly tree parts and foliage. It was a murky dark brown colour with a sheen of mist on its surface. Except where we were standing, there was no space between trees and river; the jungle seemed to melt into the water. There was a brooding, sinister atmosphere, and the river exuded a sense of foreboding. I took a step forward but Rabul stopped me.

"Crocodiles," he said, "dogs and even people have been taken."

As he spoke, the carcass of some unidentified creature floated by.

49

"Maybe a tree-climbing kangaroo. I have seen many dead animals in the water and even a body of a child once. The Ramu comes from the mountains a long way away." He turned away.

On the way back to Giri, the river dominated my thoughts, but also the weird idea of a kangaroo that could climb trees.

Over the next eighteen months, I visited the Ramu many times, and that feeling of exhilaration and nervousness was always there. It was a very special place.

Well looked after
Valuable pigs

A typical Giri family home

Manham outside
Bonnie and Hans'
House in front,
Father George's
Behind

Giri Number 1

Tobias lived on Manham Island. He had some magical powers, and he could turn himself into a pig and also into a boulder. He was also very lazy and while the other villagers were looking after their gardens, he couldn't be bothered and slept on his veranda.

At night, he would sneak out and steal food from the other gardens: yams, sweet potatoes and greens. Sometimes, he would change into a pig and lure another pig that belonged to someone else into the deep forest; then, he would change back into a man and kill the pig, cook it and gorge on the pig meat. He was too lazy to hide the bones or the remains of the fire.

People from the village were very upset when their pigs went missing; they were very valuable and used for Sing Sings. At first, they thought the pigs were just wandering off and getting lost in the forest, but then a young villager, called Abu, was out hunting and came across the remains of an old cooking fire pit with the bones of a pig.

Others in the village realised they were losing vegetables from their gardens, mainly yams, sweet potatoes and bananas.

Men and women from the village held a secret meeting. They suspected Tobias, so they did not invite him to the meeting. They decided to set a trap.

That night they hid around several gardens that had plenty of vegetables growing. Around midnight, Tobias turned up and started digging up the yams and picking the bananas in one of the gardens.

The people who were hiding jumped out, angrily shouting curses and threats. They had many weapons, including spears, knives and clubs. Tobias ran as fast as he could into the forest, and the villagers ran after him. He ran a long way and was getting very tired. He *wanted to turn into a boulder, but he could not let them see him do it.*

Just as he was running out of the energy he needed to keep going, he came across a hole that a pig had made. He threw himself into it and turned himself into a pig. It was bad luck for him that the fastest villager had been close enough to see what he did and, when he reached the hole, he shouted to the others that they should come to where he was.

They stabbed the pig with their Spears and knives over and over again and beat it with their clubs.

Tobias turned himself into a boulder, but it was too late, he was badly injured and died soon after. The villages realised their spears, knives and clubs were being broken from stabbing and hitting the boulder.

The boulder is still there, near the village of Lassa on Manam Island.

Chapter 5   The Three Horses of the Apocalypse

VSO had set up a procedure that single volunteers who were in isolated places would receive letters about once every six weeks. I believe the writers were Oxford University undergraduates, probably earning a bit of beer money doing it.

I really looked forward to receiving them; they kept me up to date with what was happening in England, including the football scores as well as any topic that the writer fancied. They were really well written. I always replied.

I'd been teaching only a few weeks when the first one arrived. As I was reading it, Bonnie bustled into my room.

"Masta, Pater I laikim yu go long haus belong em. Yumitupela go nau." (Master*, the father wants to see you. We should go now)

On arrival, Father George told me that the following Saturday, he would normally be making his monthly trip to Bogia to collect supplies and post. However, the Unimog had developed a fault and even having spent three solid days underneath, he had not been able to rectify it. I was, therefore, to go to Bogia by horse.

Now, bear in mind, Bogia was at least an eight hour horse ride and that I had never ridden a horse before. In fact, I was quite nervous of them. I knew by now that there was no point in mentioning this. The father had an uncanny knack of only hearing what he wanted to hear.

The station had three horses: two white mayors and one stallion, the colour of a red setter. They were called Giri, Toby and Red. According to the father, Giri and

Toby were tame, but Red was very wild and dangerous; even Father George had never ridden him.

My departure on Saturday morning was delayed as it took Bonnie and Hans an hour and a half to catch one of the tame horses, although I must admit Red was determined to make it as difficult as possible. He reared up alarmingly and tried to kick Bonnie and Hans a number of times, and I have to say that watching this did not fill me with confidence. Every time they came close to catching one, Red would charge in and scare the other horses off.

Eventually, Hans fetched some villagers to help and he and Bonnie separated and went for one white horse each. While Red was causing havoc with Bonnie's attempt to saddle Toby, Hans was able to catch and saddle Giri. Red managed to land a kick on Bonnie's leg, which went purple and hurt him a lot. It looked awful. Father George looked at it and declared it was badly bruised but that it wasn't broken or permanently damaged.

Hans led Giri to where I was standing. Now Hans could ride a bit and had given me the theory the evening before. Nevertheless, I must admit, it was with great fear and trepidation that I grabbed hold of the saddle and hauled myself onto the horse. I am pleased to say that I found myself facing the right way, so that was at least one possible humiliation out of the way. However, I immediately made my first and almost my last mistake. What I totally forgot was to take hold of the reins.

Bonnie, Hans and Father George were probably as surprised as I was, as the horse shot off at enormous speed in completely the wrong direction. I would say her nought to sixty acceleration would have put Ferrari to shame. I was helpless; the reins had fallen over the horse's head and I could not reach them. Truthfully, even if I had been able to grab them, there is no way I would have let go of her mane. I simply sat, leaning forward with my face hard against her neck and hung on for grim death. Fear comes nowhere to describing what I was feeling at that moment.

We hurtled around the station for about five minutes, or was it five days? At one point, a corrugated roof came within a millimetre of shaving my head off, or so the father told me, with relish, later.

Finally, she charged down the hill and I could see we were headed straight for the barbed wire fence that separated the mission station from the copra plantation. I tensed, waiting for her to jump the fence. However, she did not. Instead, she stopped, dead, three metres from the fence. There was no warning; she just went from wild gallop to dead still in a split second. I, however, did not stop. I shot like a bullet over her head, through the air and smashed into the fence, which twanged alarmingly with the impact.

I lay there, unable to move, partly because of the various parts of me that were hooked to the vicious barbs but also through a mixture of fear, relief, shock, pain and loss of blood.

I could see Father George running towards me, his face full of concern. Was he at long last going to show some emotion towards me, some compassion, maybe? He patted Giri's flank, looked down at me, frowned and said.

"If you treat my horse like that again, I will not let you ride her."

As Bonnie and Hans unhooked me and lifted me to my feet, I was crying and laughing at the same time.

Having obtained some first aid and a lecture from the father on the art of horsemanship, including a demonstration that, I must admit, made it look easy, I tried again. The main thing I learned, apart from getting hold of the reins, was that if you pulled them hard enough, the horse did not move, certainly not quickly.

We set off again, but this time, the reins were where they should be, and we were going in the right direction at a very sedate pace. In fact, considering how hard I was pulling on the reins, it was a wonder we moved at all. After a few minutes, I began to relax and was positively Cock a hoop as I jauntily rode through Giri village, waving to anyone who happened to look up and those who didn't, for that matter. Five minutes later, we came to a small river.

Being in the dry season, the river was low, less than two feet at its deepest and about ten feet wide. A rough log bridge spanned it. I rode towards the bridge and could feel the horse's unease. I could see immediately that this was not going to work; it was hopeless. There were gaps between the logs and there was no chance of Giri crossing safely. I decided this was not a problem however, we would just wade across the river. We rode to the river's edge and then stopped. I gently encouraged the horse with kind words and gentle heels. As time passed, the words became less kind and the heels less gentle. I shouted at her, implored her, and pounded on her neck with my fist. I dismounted, took hold of the reins and pulled with all my might. I went behind her and pushed. I went down on my knees and begged her. We remained stationary. I have to admit, I cried with frustration but Giri had no compassion. She remained unmoved.

An hour and a half after leaving the mission, I rode back in. I felt dejected, defeated and humiliated. Hans and Bonnie looked up at me and would not meet my eye. Watching from his balcony, Father George shook his head and went inside his house.

I went straight to my room, leaving Bonnie to deal with the horse. My face was red with embarrassment, but also, a determination was building in me based on anger and shame. I sat and thought about what to do and eventually, the outline of a plan began to form in my mind. I walked down to Giri Village.

Early the following day, Hans and I saddled the horse. It had been tethered overnight to make for a quick getaway, so while the father was presiding over early morning mass and no one was about, I rode quietly out of the station.

Giri and I arrived at the river and stopped. I spent several minutes trying to get her to move forward but she was not to be persuaded. I gave the signal. Four young people ran out of the bush behind us, each carrying a burning branch. Yelling and shouting, they charged at our rear. The horse panicked and dashed across the river. Horse 0 Human 1 (I refuse to count the previous day!)

The boys and girls followed me to the next river but there was no problem; Giri crossed without a fuss, and I paid them off with chocolate bars and some pages from an old newspaper for each of them. I then rode into the sunset, or something like that anyway.

The rest of the journey was like a kid's dream come true. I was John Wayne hunting baddies. I was Sir Lancelot rescuing the damsel in distress. I was a champion jockey winning The Derby.

We rode over hills, through valleys, across rivers. In the few small communities that we passed through, children would run out of their homes and chase us, cheering and old folk would stare. And yes, I did shout Yee Haa! many times.

I cannot say I had complete control over her. On hilly sections, she would gallop down one side with just enough momentum to gain the summit of the next. She would then stop and chew grass for a minute or two before setting off again. One time I dismounted for a pee and Giri took off without me. I caught up with her at the summit of the next hill. I didn't care, I had won.

On reaching Bogia, I had some time to kill as we would not be returning until the following day and Giri needed time to rest. I wandered down to the sea and, as there was nobody about and I was rather sore from my many hours riding, I stripped down to my shorts and enjoyed an hour of frolicking in the water. It was a beautiful evening and the sea was calm and warm.

I was thinking about coming out when I saw a young man and a woman shouting at me. I waded towards the shore and, trying to be as polite as possible, they told me I should leave the water as this part of the coast was notorious for sea crocodiles and I was fortunate not to have been attacked.

I had never heard of sea crocodiles and wondered if they were playing a joke. However, later I heard that they were right and in the past, people who had come to collect salt water for cooking had been taken, even though they were only in the shallows. Apparently, crocodiles are not only fast in the water but on land as well.

The following day I rode back into Giri Mission. It felt as though there should have been a brass band playing. Of course, there wasn't, I received no praise, and in fact, the only thing the father said was that I had forgotten to get him a copy of his newspaper. It didn't matter to me; I was able to enjoy the achievement for myself. I did write to my mum and dad about it, though.

I must explain my payment to the youngsters from the village who helped Giri and me cross the river. The mission had a small store which opened on a Sunday but only for those who had attended mass. Often payment was made with goods or labour rather than money. I was surprised to see people buying single pages from newspapers, particularly broadsheets. After all, nobody could speak English, let alone read the Daily Telegraph.

In fact, these were used to wrap tobacco for smoking. A huge cigarette would be created which would last all day and, when not being smoked, would live behind the ear. Apparently, The Sunday Times provided the best smoke.

* Bonnie called Father George and me, Master. I am unsure where he picked it up, as I didn't hear anyone else use the term. I was not really aware of its connotations at the time but, nevertheless, I didn't like it. Hans called me Richard and I tried very hard to get Bonnie to do the same. He always gave me a huge grin and agreed wholeheartedly, but the next time I was Master once again. I'm sure it was not deliberate, he just forgot. Occasionally he half remembered and came out with Masta Richard.

Daboo told me this story in 1969 during a visit to Bogia.

Daboo was very old. He worked at the mission in Bogia as a gardener although he could hardly bend and spent most of his time smoking his pipe and watching the world go by. The priest kept him on as he had nowhere else to go; he had come as an orphan many years before.

He told me of the time he met the Queen of England in Madang. He had decided to go to Madang as he had never been to a big village before. He had stowed away on a copra boat but the crew had found him, tied a rope around his belly and thrown overboard. They had towed him all the way. When he arrived, he was wet and cold.

He was very hungry, so he went to the church to see if the priest would give him some food. When he went in, he could hear music. There was no one there except for the Queen of England; she was playing the organ and was very good.

"I asked her if she had any food. She gave me something strange but tasty. She said it was a cheese sandwich. I asked her where The King was, and she said she didn't have a king, only a prince called Philip.

Someone came into the church and said something to her and she told me that she had to go and watch some schoolchildren dancing. She said if I ever came to England, I should visit her at Buckingham Palace in London, and she would make me another cheese sandwich. She was very nice."

The Queen first visited New Guinea in 1974.

Chapter 6   The School

Two of the teachers, Johan and Philip, had left at the end of the previous term. Leo and Venansius arrived for the beginning of the new school year. Venansius was the new headteacher but would also teach a class as we had more children coming. He was a fantastic leader and teacher, and everyone was pleased to welcome him.

Some evenings, they got together and sang songs from their homelands. Several of them played guitar and percussion. After a while, I was invited to join them and I think they appreciated the fact that I was not pushy and did not try to take part; I was just happy to listen.

John Pious became my special friend. He was a man who was quick to smile and had simple needs. He lived with his wife and baby. The others shared bachelor huts.

To become teachers, they should have completed primary school, one or two years of high school and one or two years of teacher training. John had not made it to teacher training and was only allowed to teach because of a shortage. He was constantly afraid he would lose his job if a more qualified person applied. The staff were reservedly friendly towards me; none of them had ever had a white colleague before.

There were thirty eight pupils in my class from seven different villages, although I rarely had more than thirty on any given day as they were often needed to do chores in their villages, particularly the girls. Their ages ranged from nine to fifteen years old and they had all done two years of education. Twelve of them boarded from Monday to Friday as they lived a long way away.

There were two boarding houses, boys and girls. They were quite large, and the children slept in rows, on palm leaves. This is what they would have done at home. The father provided each of them with a thin blanket, although this was rarely needed.

The borders were very self-sufficient, they brought their own food to last the week, and usually, the children from each village would share and cook for each other. They were also responsible for keeping their huts clean, and, for their own hygiene. It seemed to work, I was never aware of any problems in all the time I was there, which I find remarkable.

Children from Arengin, the village furthest away, had to walk three to six hours on a Sunday afternoon to get to school, depending on the conditions, and the same on the way back on a Friday afternoon. Sadly, once some of the girls reached the age of fifteen, or sometimes even younger, they were eligible to get married and were expected to work in their villages. Their attendance stopped or, at the very least, was inconsistent.

After the parade and the singing of the national anthem, the morning was spent studying English, maths and religious education. All pupils studied a defined national curriculum in these subjects.

In the afternoons, subjects that were considered less important were covered; geography and history but also the curriculum was less rigid. Often, we went out into the bush for nature study, we would wander around and I would test the children's knowledge of the plant, bird and animal life. Naturally, I had no idea of

63

the correct answers, and although the pupils learned very little, I learned lots. On other afternoons I would tell them about life in England or tell them stories; Cinderella was one of their favourites, or they told traditional New Guinea tales. Unfortunately, many of their stories were quite violent. They also talked about their lives and hopes for the future.

I would describe my class as a motley collection; most of them had no footwear and wore hand me down clothes that were torn and ragged, usually just a pair of shorts and a T-shirt for the boys and a sari or simple skirt and T-shirt for the girls and that was about it. They were cheerful, cheeky, quick to laugh and eager to learn. It took about five minutes for me to realise that I loved them all. Nevertheless, I remembered my VSO instructions; start off firm, establish good discipline and then you can relax. I was strict and would allow no nonsense.

Boy's boarding house
My motley but beautiful class

A man and his wife went into the bush to find sweet potatoes and yams. The woman had magical powers, but she used them only for good. They saw a young wild boar that had impaled itself on a branch and was squealing, obviously in great pain and distress. The woman went to the animal and removed the branch. She then used her powers and healed its wound, and the boar ran off into the bush.

Her husband was angry. He had wanted to kill the creature and take it home to eat. He attacked his wife with his spear and tried to kill her. She flew up into a tree and watched him. He threw his spear, but it hit the trunk of the tree and stuck fast.

The earth around the base of the tree was wet and had many colours due to the different minerals in the soil; yellows, Browns, Reds and greens. He picked up clods of earth and through them, hitting her on the body and face.

The woman decided she did not want to live with people anymore and would live with the birds. So she took off, using the new wings she had grown. Her body and wings became the colour of the earth that had been thrown at her. And so, she became the first of her kind.

The man returned to the village and, spitefully, told everyone that he had seen a new type of bird called a bird of paradise. It was colourful, and its feathers would make good head dresses for Sing Sings and other celebrations. If they saw one, they should shoot it with their bows and arrows.

That is why the bird of paradise lives at the very top of the forest canopy and is rarely seen.

Chapter 7   The Road

Village men would get together in a large building called a house for men (hausman) or meeting house (haus kibung).   Every village I visited had one. It was long and wide with a thatched roof and low thatched walls.

Meetings would be held there and decisions concerning the village taken.   Women and children would congregate outside and sometimes one of the women would shout her opinion.   The men always listened attentively. Although some of the discussions were heated, people did not interrupt each other and, in the end, decisions were taken by consensus.

The problem for me was that the debates took place at an enormous pace, in a mixture of tok pisin and the local language, which was very hard to follow.

A man's status depended on his age, his wisdom and the number of pigs he owned.   High status men were known as village elders.

At other times men gathered in the evening just to share stories and gossip.

Bachelors were allowed to sleep in the meeting house temporarily if they had nowhere else to go.

I believe in all the local villages, but certainly in Giri, there was a real sense of community. If a young couple got married for instance, the whole village would turn out to build a house for them and help clear the bush for their vegetable garden. It tended to take a long time however, people from Giri certainly did not like to be rushed.

In many villages, men had more than one wife. It did happen in Giri but was relatively rare.

It was common for families to share children. Those who had more than they really wanted would give one or more to families with less or none. However, it was done with the understanding that if the original parents were not happy with a child's upbringing, they could take him or her back.

Sundays were my favourite days. I would get up and go to early morning mass. Afterwards, the store would be opened, and I would help serve. Those who had money that had been sent to them from relatives who had found work in Madang, or had done some work for the father, would buy small tins of fish or meat, a few manufactured cigarettes, maybe some newspaper or even an item of clothing if they were feeling really flush.

Once the store closed, the day's big event would begin; the weekly soccer match (or massacre, as I called it) between Giri Number 1; my team and Giri Number 2, which included the other teachers. The pitch was huge, rough and sloped; the ball was like worst quality steel and definitely not spherical. The players, of which any number could be on each side, wore only shorts. There was no easy way of distinguishing one team from the other.

The first time I participated, I played barefoot, as did everyone. I kicked the ball only once, and retired with, what felt like, multiple fractures of the toes. The second time, I played in shoes and dashed around heroically. I was helped off after twenty minutes with heat stroke.

After that, I was a little more careful. I still find it difficult to believe the distances the ball would be kicked and some of the tackles would make Vinny Jones flinch.

The matches were taken very seriously and I think a few grudges were settled on the pitch. However, the result of the game was irrelevant; neither side knew how many goals they or their opponents had scored, nor did they care.

The games were punctuated by smoke and drinks breaks. Green coconuts were brought out; this is the stage before they go brown as we see them, the milk is drunk, and the soft flesh is eaten using bamboo scoops. It has a wonderful taste and texture.

Having survived the match, I would wander into one of the villages to yarn. The evening was generally spent with the other teachers, and we would while away the night swapping stories, singing and laughing. Nothing serious was ever discussed.

I have always been in awe of talented people or people in authority, from the local copper to great musicians. The staff of Giri School were pleasantly awesome. They laughed and acted as if they didn't have a care in the world. They played slide guitar or percussion expertly and were loved by most of the community, children and adults alike. I wanted to be like them.

One Sunday afternoon, I was sitting with John and his family and I mentioned that I had noticed in the villages that there was always red paint on the ground and on the bottom of the stilts on which the houses were built. I had also seen that many villagers had red stained teeth and spat something red from their mouths. I asked John to explain. He laughed.

"Poroman (Means partner or friend but can also mean foolish person), not paint, beetle nuts; that's what causes the red everywhere. I will show you."

He went into his house and brought out some green nuts, sort of spherical and over an inch in diameter, green leaves and a tin containing a white powder. He gave me one of the nuts.

"Now, put it in your mouth, bite it, get out the nut inside and spit out the husk. Chew the nut but do not swallow. Like this."

I copied him and grimaced. It was a strange taste, very bitter with a chalky texture.

"At the same time, dip a leaf into the powder and chew that with the nut. When your mouth has a lot of juice, spit it out over the side."

I did as he said, and my spit was bright red. I also spat out the nut. It was not a pleasant experience.

The beetle nut is actually the seed of the areca palm, and the powder is lime, made by scraping shells. I never did find out what the leaf was, but I think many things can be used.

Betel nuts give a mild high, similar to a very strong coffee. Many people in Papua New Guinea use them. Taken too often, they are supposed to be harmful. In time, I got to like chewing betel nuts.

At the beginning of the Easter holiday, Father George said he wanted me to build a road. He said he could not do it himself because he was too busy. All through February and March, he had been fully involved in building new classrooms. The work was done by local villagers under his supervision. He was often away with the Unimog collecting materials from Bogia.

We walked to the spot about three miles from the mission. At that point, the present track sloped down to the edge of a river, followed the river for about a hundred yards and climbed back up again. The ground was often waterlogged and thick with mud along the side of the river. Even in the dry season, the Unimog often got stuck and had to be winched up. I was to dig into the side of the hill so the road would be level all the way through.

My mind started churning out the many problems associated with this project and why I should not be entrusted with it, but by the time I got to the point of mentioning a few of them to Father George, he was already walking home. I finally caught up with him on his veranda, but before I could say a word, he showed me a diagram that he said would explain everything and remove all my misgivings.

This is a reproduction.

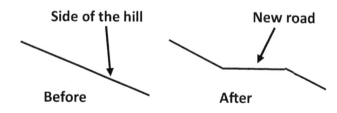

Simple Really!

Ten villagers were employed to do the digging and I was told to complete it within one week, otherwise it would cost too much. It turned out that two of the diggers had done similar work before and knew the best way of going about it. That was good as I was clueless and Father George had been somewhat vague on the nitty-gritty of how it should be done.

On the first day, we worked for about half an hour, after which they all downed tools and sat down for twenty minutes for a rest and a drink. This pattern continued for the whole morning.

After lunch, I asserted my authority and told them we would work for two hours solid, with no breaks. They all nodded their agreement. After half an hour, they all downed tools and sat down for a rest and a drink. I decided to show my displeasure by continuing to work and embarrass them. After another half hour, I collapsed with heatstroke and had to lie down in the shade for an hour.

That evening, I thought about what had to be done and soon realised there was absolutely no chance of finishing the road in the allotted time unless things changed. The following morning, I offered them a deal. Although I was a volunteer, I was actually paid five Australian dollars a month. Since there was nothing to spend it on, I had accrued thirty dollars. I offered to pay each of them an extra two dollars out of my own money and five pages from The Sunday Times if they could finish on time. This changed everything. The oldest member of the group, Aluicious, took charge. His first order was to tell me not to help but to go and sit in the shade as I was a liability; harsh but fair, and I was secretly very relieved. They completed the job on the seventh day as darkness fell.

The following morning, I accompanied Father George to see it for himself. We took the Unimog and drove along the new section without any mishaps.

I thought maybe he would name it Richard's Road, Masters' Motorway or, at the very least, accept that I had finally done something of which he approved. He looked at it for a while, nodded and drove home without saying a word.

I didn't care; I was ecstatic and when the new term started, I took my class to see the road and based all my lessons on it for a week. Not only that, but for a few mornings when I took the register, instead of each saying, 'Good morning, Mr Masters' they had to say, 'Good morning, Great Road Builder.' They all found this highly amusing.

My moment of glory was only spoilt when one of the girls, Aluicious' granddaughter Abigail, stood up and said accusingly.

"My grandad said they did all the work, and you just sat there and watched."

I explained to her in a patient way that leadership was about planning and organising; it is done with the brain, not with the shovel. I also made a mental note to give the little devil a hard time for the rest of the term.

At the beginning of April, we moved into the new classrooms and the old ones were dismantled. To be honest, teaching in them was not much different except when we had heavy rain. The noise on the corrugated metal roofs meant the only way to be heard was to shout. The pupils had great fun pretending they couldn't hear anything that involved telling them to do some work.

The classrooms were built in pairs, with a room between the two teaching areas. One of these became my new office, home and sleeping quarters.

Villagers come together   Sunday morning soccer
to build a house for a
newly married couple
with spectator support

The new classrooms

Two brothers lived in a village. One was a good man and one was a bad man. They both wanted to marry a girl in the next village. She liked the good man, she did not like the bad man. She agreed to marry the good man and her parents invited him to come and eat with them. When they had finished eating, they said he could stay in their house until morning as it was too late for him to go home. He went out for a short walk.

His brother, the bad man, had followed him to the house and when he saw him go out for a walk, he attacked him and beat him over the head with a rock until he was dead. He hid his body in a concealed cave. Once it was completely dark, he went back to the house and lay down in the place the parents had put aside for his brother. When everybody was asleep, he quietly went over and lay next to the girl. In the morning the parents saw the man sleeping with their daughter and were angry, they called her bad names and told her she was no longer welcome in the family home. They sent her away with the bad man. She had nowhere to go so she had to agree to marry him. After a year they had a child, a son. The bad brother loved his son very much. One night, in a dream she saw what had happened when the bad brother had killed the good brother and lay down with her in the hut.

She took her son and hid him in the forest. In the bag she normally used to carry him, she put some large stones. She went to find the bad brother, her husband. "I know what you did to your brother," she said, "and I'm going to punish you."

She threw the bag with the stones into the nearby river. The man cried out and rushed into the river to save his son, but the river was flowing very fast and he was swept away and died.

The woman married another man and was pleased that she was no longer married to the bad man. She and her son had a happy life.

Chapter 8   Sing Sing

People in the villages around Giri had always revered, perhaps even worshipped, their ancestors. Even in the late sixties and despite the coming of Christianity, their ancestors were like gods to many.   They were respected, and, importantly, there were lines of communication to gain information and ask for help. If the ancestors were upset, bad things could happen to individuals or even to the whole village.

In some villages, a ritual takes place when a man who has at least one son dies. His family builds a wooden box with a solid base, and the body is placed in it. The box is taken to the family vegetable garden and placed on stilts about eight feet high. A small hole is cut in the centre of the base and a ceremonial wooden dish is put on the ground directly underneath the hole.   Over many months, the body slowly decomposes and the juices from it drip through the hole into the bowl below.

When the dish is fairly full, the transfer ceremony takes place where the oldest son of the deceased drinks the contents of the bowl. This allows him to receive the wisdom, knowledge and magic powers of his father and gain his ancestors' approval.

Sing Sing is a festival of music and dance and happens throughout Papua New Guinea in different forms. It represents the culture and beliefs of the area in which it takes place. I looked forward to my first Sing Sing with great anticipation. Teaching was hard in the days before as the children were incredibly excited; some of the older ones would be taking part for the first time.

On the morning of the festival, some of the village pigs were killed and prepared for cooking. Yams and taros were harvested, and sago was readied.

The men who were participating began the long process of getting everything ready. This particular event was to honour and ask for favour from their ancestors and to celebrate the sun and the moon.

Early afternoon, before the rains came, the feast took place. In the centre of the village, huge wooden bowls were laid out on the ground and in the centre of each one was pig and other meats: rodents, grubs and some whose origin I didn't really want to think about. Around this were vegetables, which included sago, yam, sweet potato and greens. About twenty men and older boys sat around each bowl and every person had a wooden spoon. The feast began and everyone plunged in.

Being English, I, of course, waited for everyone else to take their first spoonful and then, not wanting anyone to think I was greedy or bad-mannered, I took a small piece of pork and a slither of yam and chewed carefully before swallowing. I may have come from a poor working class background but I still knew my table manners. I turned back to the platter to observe the last morsel being devoured.

Another lesson learnt: when you share food with others, you shovel it down your gullet as quickly as possible, or you go hungry.

After the men had finished and left, the women, girls and younger children sat down to eat. Their food was different, and I noticed that the meat was fatty off-cuts and bones, hardly any lean meat at all.

Following the feast, the men marked their faces with symbols. They used paints gleaned from plants but also soils, including red ochre, clays and chalk. Both the colours and the symbols had meaning; black, for instance, was used to ward off evil. These secrets and skills were passed down from generation to generation.

Extravagant headdresses were used with exotic bird feathers reaching up towards the sky, and necklaces of teeth and shells were worn around the neck and on the wrists. Some men rubbed red ochre all over their skin, and others had fish bones piercing their noses. They wore grass skirts and no other clothing; the skirts were dyed in a range of earthy colours. It was the most amazing and colourful sight.

The women and children also wore grass skirts and necklaces similar to the men; some painted their bodies. However, they did not paint their faces and their heads were bare.

The Sing Sing began at dusk, either inside the meeting house or sometimes outside in the centre of the village. The area where it took place was lit by torches made from brushwood but also some lanterns bought from the mission shop. The music rhythms were made by five or six men beating kundus. These were handheld drums made from hollowed out sections of tree trunks and skins. They had pictures and symbols scratched into them. The dancers were in lines three abreast, about thirty in all. They shuffled backwards and forwards to the rhythm, sometimes chanting sounds and words that complemented the drums. After a while, the dance would come to an end with a crescendo of sound from the drums, a dramatic move forward and a yell from the dancers.

There would be a pause for a smoke, a drink, and, of course, a betel nut. One or two dancers and drummers dropped out, and others joined in, and then the whole thing would start again with a slightly different rhythm and movement.

A short way off, the women and children were doing their own version, dancing to the drumbeat. However, the movements were far more animated and less ritualistic. I was not allowed to join in with the men, but the women were happy for me to participate. It was not as easy as I had anticipated, and I heard quite a few giggles at my awkwardness, but I loved every minute of it.

It went on for hours and you would be forgiven for thinking it must have become tedious but that was not the case. I attended four Sing Sings in all and not only did I enjoy every moment, but I always had a sense of being part of something very special; I was at the heart of a culture that, perhaps, in the not too distant future, would be gone forever.

Watching and moving to the beat with all those extraordinary people made me feel part of something unique. I feel so privileged to have been there.

Preparing for Sing Sing – Giri Number 1

Preparing for Sing Sing – Giri Number 1

Dobari was a large village in the Highlands, a day's walk from Mount Piora. Over five hundred men and women lived in or near the village. The men of the village were very cruel and often publicly punished their wives and children by humiliating them. They would beat them or make them walk around naked. Some women and children died because of the injuries they received.

Dari was an older woman whose husband was crueller than most. She decided she was going to leave her husband, run away and fend for herself. Over a long period of time, she secretly told the other women of her plan; every one of them wanted to go with her.

One day, the men were all at the meeting house. The women knew they would be there for hours, so they collected their children and a few possessions, including knives and axes, and quietly left the village. They walked into the bush, heading west all the time. It was not easy; there were many gorges and mountains in their way. Sometimes, they followed rivers, walking in the water so the dogs from Dabori couldn't follow their scent. At the end of the tenth day, they entered a forest and, deep inside, found a flat piece of land with no trees growing. There was a stream flowing nearby. They decided this was where they would live. It was perfect for their needs.

Over the next year, they made gardens and built simple houses. They were very happy and brought their children up to be kind and gentle and to respect each other. They did not hunt and never ate meat. They only ate the vegetables and fruits that they grew or found. They used fungi, herbs and plants for medicine.

The wild animals and birds in the area realised that the women were no danger to them and would come into the village, where they were helped if they had thorns or illnesses. The women would encourage their children to stroke them and play with them.

Most of the children that had run away with their mothers were content with their life but one of them Jammu, who was now fifteen, was always moaning about things. One day, he killed a pigeon, cooked and ate it. The women were very cross and a meeting was held. The decision was taken to banish him from the village and he was told to leave and never come back.

This turned out to be a mistake, as after nearly two months, he found his way back to Dabori. He told the men about the women and said he would lead them to the new village, which he did. When they arrived, they charged in and ruthlessly tied up the women and sat them in the centre of the village.

Dari's Husband was their leader and told the women what was going to happen to them.

"Firstly, we are going to burn your village. Secondly, we will take you back to Dabori and each of you will be beaten. Thirdly, you will not be allowed to talk to anyone except your husband and when he is not with you, you will be tied up. We are going to make you regret running away."

He stopped as he could hear strange noises all around him and when the men looked, they saw many animals coming out of the bush on all sides: wild boar, cassowaries, wild dogs, quoll and rats. The sky above was filled with birds. The animals and birds attacked the men who tried to escape into the bush. Meanwhile, the rats chewed through the women's ropes and freed them.

Not one man was left alive to return to Dabori. Their bodies were burnt and the ashes cast into the stream without ceremony.

It is said that the women still live in their secret haven to this very day.

Chapter 9   Dangerous Creatures in the Month of May.

One evening in May, I went to Giri Number 2 on a political errand. Father George had asked me to visit a man called Eric Basala. He was a very important village elder with a great deal of influence. The father wanted me to attempt to bribe him into allowing some of the village land that boarded the mission to be used to extend our copra plantation. I could offer him goods from the store, a small amount of money or I could offer to be his son. Apparently, having a white man as your son was all the rage.

All had gone well. I now had three sets of parents and had agreed to visit him and his family once a week to eat and spend some time with them. Each visit I would bring some newspaper and a few tins of fish. Also, on the following Sunday, I had arranged for him to come to the store to kit himself out with a brand new shirt, socks, sandals and a pair of shorts.

I had noticed that many of the men in Giri number 2 had patterns on their skin, like small dark rectangles in lines where the skin was lifted. Eric had lots of them; they were very obvious. I asked him about them.

"In the old days, when you reached a certain age and became a man, you were taken to a hut, and a village elder would cut your skin with sharp bamboo knives; they would often make them into the shape of a crocodile or other creatures." He removed his shirt to show me an amazing crocodile on his back and buttocks. "There would be hundreds of these cuts all over your body. It took many hours and was very painful and some men fainted. I did not. It still happens when someone wants it done but you had no choice in my day."

On returning to the mission, I went to my classroom to prepare for the following day's lessons. I was startled to see in the corner a snake coiled up. It was completely still and appeared to be dead. My fellow teachers were not averse to playing the odd trick on me and I was fairly sure that this was one of their jolly japes. I took a close look at it; it was about eighteen inches long and striped brown and beige. I decided I would play them at their own game; I would take it to Leo's classroom and leave it in his desk drawer. He was the primary trickster. As I put my hand out to pick it up, I hesitated. OK, I was pretty sure it was a joke, but shouldn't I make absolutely sure? I went to the next classroom, where the other teachers had congregated.

"OK, which of you left the dead snake in my room? Come on, own up."

They all looked at me as if I was mad.

"Show me," said Venansius.

As we walked into the room, the snake could be seen slithering over one of the low walls and was gone. It would not be an exaggeration to say I was somewhat shocked.

"Hec," I said, "I nearly picked it up; I thought you guys were playing a trick."

Venansius smiled, "That, poroman, was a death adder, one of our more deadly snakes, as you might gather from the name. Had you touched it, you would have undoubtedly been bitten, and you would be well on your way to heaven or the other place, of course. Oh, and you would have died in agony." He tousled my hair and left.

I was really shaken; I knew how close I had come. John put his arm around me and led me to his house. He helped calm me down with a betel nut and a cigarette.

After that, whenever I went to my classroom, I always tentatively put my head through the window first to check I had no visitors. The other teachers found this highly amusing.

Quite often, in the late afternoon, the sky would go dark, almost black, and torrential rain would fall, the like of which I had never experienced before. It would crash down, making an extraordinary noise like continuous thunder. It usually lasted between one and two hours. It was welcome and cooled everything down.

When there was no rain, the heat built up and became very oppressive and uncomfortable. On those days, after school, some of the village children would go to a small river not far from Giri Number 1, for a swim. The river was about twelve yards wide and, eventually, many miles downstream, flowed into the Ramu. Sometimes, we teachers would join them. There were some rocks overlooking a place where the water was nice and deep and we would have diving or silly jumping competitions. The kids loved us being there.

The Saturday following the snake event, I was feeling particularly hot and bothered. I thought I would go for a swim before lunch. I put on a pair of old shorts and wandered down to the river.

I stood on the rocks for some time, looking at the bush on the other side; it was beautiful; there were so many shades of green and brown and many sounds from birds and animals which I didn't recognise: a Symphony of New Guinea. I was mesmerised and totally relaxed and at peace.

Finally, I returned to the real world and looked down, ready to jump. At that moment, a crocodile floated lazily below me, followed by a second one. It would be fair to say I was surprised and shaken by this turn of events and quickly decided to leave the area as I was well aware that crocodiles were not only quick in water but could also run pretty fast on land. I tried not to think of what would have happened if the view across the river had been less riveting.

On my way back to Giri, I passed the garden where several women were tending crops. I told them about my experience with the crocodiles and asked how it was they let their children swim there in the evenings.

They smiled and replied, "san wara i belong long pukpuk, apinun, wara I belong long manmari alsam." (Daytime, the river belongs to the crocodiles but in the evening, the river belongs to the people)

It was a wonderful answer and so typical of the people's attitude towards nature and wildlife. My only worry was, had anyone told the crocodiles?

On the last Sunday in May, papa belong me, Joseph Huri, came to see me. He told me that some of the village men were going hunting in the afternoon and he had asked them if they would take me along. I was reluctant; I did not really like the idea of hunting and killing animals. He pointed out that larger game were rare in the area and they probably wouldn't find anything worth hunting anyway. He said I should experience it at least once as it was a great honour being allowed to go with them. This was rather pleasing and good for my ego or would have been had he not spoilt it by saying that they had said no at first and had only agreed when he promised that I would give them lots of newspaper.

We met outside the village, nine of us all together. The first thing they did was rub mud on my legs, arms, face and my genuine Millets jungle hat, which tragically never recovered. Stella would have been devastated. Fortunately, my shorts and shirt were dark, or I'm sure they would have done those as well.

We crept through the thick undergrowth of the forest in single file; I was near the front. The others were barefooted and silent. Despite wearing shoes, I was pleased with myself for being as quiet as they were until the leader, Pedro, stopped and walked back towards me.

"Richard, you are making more noise than two rutting zoncas. The animals will hear you and be gone long before we get them in sight."

He walked back with me to the last man and signalled for me to keep walking. Every time I stopped and turned, he signalled me to go further. He was not satisfied until I was about thirty yards behind the rest. I felt just a touch cross and humiliated.

At one point, I thought I glimpsed a cassowary through the trees, but it sensed my presence and was gone. I didn't tell the others; of course, It might have been my imagination.

After a few hours, Pedro signalled us to be still. I was told to stay where I was. The others crept forward. I could not really see what was happening, but I heard a yelp and shouts. They beckoned me forward and told me that they had seen a wild boar feeding. They had thrown spears at it, but there was no hope of killing or even injuring it; it was too far away, but they hoped that one of the spears would draw blood and would allow them to track it. It appeared to have worked, and the tracker went to the front. Slowly and carefully, we followed its spore.

As expected, the creature had returned to its nest. Yes, wild boars build nests on the ground, with grass, branches and, basically, anything else they can find. They crawl in and are very well concealed. As we gathered together, I could see the nest about fifty yards away; it was huge. I could hear a faint grunting noise.

I still find this difficult to believe, but this was the plan. We each had two throwing Spears. With these, we were to creep to a point about fifteen yards from the nest so that we were surrounding it. We had to be beside a tree with a sturdy branch about shoulder height. At the signal, we were to throw the first spear at the nest. The wild boar would almost certainly be hurt and very angry and dangerous. It would burst out of the nest and charge at the first person it saw.

I was warned that it could easily kill you if it got to you with its tusks. The person it was charging at had to let it get to within a few yards before reacting.

He spoke in a whisper. "Make sure you have your spear poised in one hand and a firm grip on the branch with the other. Lift yourself off the ground using the branch, and as the boar passes underneath, spear it between the eyes or in the neck." He turned to me. "You do know which way round to hold the spear when you throw it?"

A little cruel and unnecessary, I felt. I nodded in what I hoped was a dignified manner.

Now, to be brutally honest, I could see one or two flaws in this plan but was given no time to express them. I chose a tree and waited. The signal was given, and I threw my spear towards the nest. I missed by miles, and had I been capable of throwing it harder, I probably would have killed one of the other hunters.

The other spears hit their target, however. There was a ferocious noise, a mixture of screams and roars. And there it was. Standing still, searching avidly for a target.

An image of my mum and dad flashed through my mind and a feeling of regret that no girl would be devastated by my passing. Because at that point, I knew, without a shadow of a doubt, I knew it was going to come for me.

I do not remember much about the next few moments. Only staring in horror at its immense size, its deadly tusks and most of all, its eyes. I looked into those small, round, black eyes that radiated hatred and venom and saw only one thing, death. It stared at me for a few seconds and then charged.

You may or may not be surprised to hear that I did not grab hold of the branch, nor did I lift myself athletically and gracefully off the ground, nor did I spear it between the eyes. I stood frozen in fear and shock. My body and mind shut down, preparing for the simple fact that I was about to die. Just as it was about to crash into me, there was a whoosh sound, and the wild boar lay dead on the ground at my feet, a spear through its neck. I also fell to the floor, shaking and shocked.

That evening, I told Joseph about what had happened and asked if I should give a present to the man who saved my life. He laughed.

"He wasn't saving your life," he said, "he was making sure that his dinner didn't get away."

The boar was cooked that evening, and many villagers shared the meat. I did not have any. I was still in shock, and being involved in the killing of an animal was really upsetting. For once in my life, I had no appetite.

Why did I include this story, after all, I am very much opposed to hunting and support many animal charities. I abhor the terrible torture that human beings inflict on creatures of all kinds.

I have heard stories of horrible cruelty to animals in parts of New Guinea. However, in the area I lived, worked and visited, I never saw a New Guinean person deliberately hurt any animal, wild or domesticated. Animals were killed to eat or for deep cultural purposes. Around Giri, allowing an animal to suffer was not countenanced; it was not in their psyche as far as I could see. When I consider the terrible way civilised societies, including our own, treat some farm animals, particularly pigs and chickens, I would find it difficult to criticise the hunters of Giri.

To this day, I have never found out what a zonca is. None of the teachers knew, nor is it used in the local language or tok pisin. I have tried Googling it and even asked at the Natural History Museum, to no avail.

Giri Number 2 – Me and Papa Number 3

In a village on the Ramu River a few miles from Giri Number 2, there was a married couple who had two children, a boy and a girl.

The children worked very hard in the garden, as well as fetching water and firewood and cleaning and cooking. One day the children were working in the garden tending sweet potatoes. They were very hungry. They went back to their house and asked their father and mother if they could have a sweet potato. Their father and mother told them to go back to work and did not give them any food.

So they went back to work but after another hour, they were so hungry they went back to their house and asked again for something to eat as they were so very hungry. Their father was angry and shouted at them.

"You're always talking about food and complaining of being hungry."

Their mother beat them and thrust some bamboos into their hand.

"Go to the stream and fill these and hurry up; there is still lots more work to do."

When they got to the stream, the little girl sat down and started crying. She told her brother she was very hungry and upset. Her brother was also hungry and upset, but he decided to try and cheer his sister up.

He changed himself into a dog and did some tricks, he rolled over and jumped in the air but she did not stop crying.

He then transformed himself into a fish and swam up and down the stream but she still did not stop crying.

Finally, he changed himself into a giant bird. He flew into the sky and around her head and gently pecked her cheek. She looked at the bird, and slowly, she stopped crying and began to smile.

She threw the bamboos to the floor and changed herself into a bird as well. Together they flew away.

Sometime later, the mother said to the father,

"Where are those lazy children? They should be back by now. I will beat them when I see them."

They walked down to the river and found the bamboos. They then searched for their children. They wondered if they had been taken by someone or had run away. Perhaps, they had fallen into the river and drowned.

They realised they had treated them very badly and that they really loved them and wanted them back.

They never saw them again, and now in the villages in that area, if children ever ask for food, the parents always give it to them and never refuse.

Chapter 10   Cargo Cult, Payback and Sanguma

Ancestors are revered in many areas of New Guinea. The people believe that they can be contacted and are able to pass messages to their children through various mediums. Many Sing Sings are to celebrate and show respect to the family members who have passed away through the generations.

What I'm about to describe will be hard for anyone to believe. It is, without a doubt, one of the strangest and most disturbing events I've ever experienced. If it was a trick, I cannot explain how it could have been staged or why.

One Saturday afternoon, I wandered down to Giri Number 1, and was surprised to find that almost the whole population was gathered in the village centre. All around me were men with painted faces, and there was an air of expectancy. At first, I thought it must be a Sing Sing of some kind but I had never heard of them being held during the day. Certainly, something was about to happen.

I could see they were not comfortable with me being around and asking questions, so I went and stood to the side with the children.

In front of the crowd was a garamut. A garamut is a drum made from the trunk of a tree. It can be up to several yards long and there is a deep slit cut into it. It is hit with a long pole, producing a deep, resonant sound that can be heard a fair distance away. As you hit it along its length the sound changes slightly.

It can be used as entertainment, but its primary function is for people to communicate with each other from afar through a complex code of beats and rhythms. Very few people in the villages would have a full knowledge and mastery of the code, but they can understand the beats for their own name or simple commands. Put it simply, it is the local telephone system, and many people have the equivalent of their own number.

The crowd went silent as a young man came forward, took the pole in his hands, and started beating the drum with a slow rhythm. A shiver went down my spine. There was something disturbing, almost mystical about the sound, and the whole atmosphere around us felt oppressive.

After some time, the beater dropped the pole but another man was there ready to catch it before it reached the floor and to continue the rhythm but at a slightly faster pace. This was repeated about twenty times, and each time somebody replaced the beater, the rhythm quickened slightly.

Many of the people watching were making strange guttural sounds, following the beat of the drum and moving their bodies in time to the rhythm. Each time a new participant took the pole, the rhythm altered slightly and the intensity of the sound increased.

After an hour, the drum was being hit at such a fast rate that it seemed impossible. Having passed on the pole, some beaters fell to the ground with exhaustion.

The last person to take the pole was an old man, a well-respected and knowledgeable village elder, surely, he could not maintain the pace. He managed for perhaps a bit longer than thirty seconds, and then something extraordinary took place. I could clearly see that his hands had stopped all movement, yet the pole continued to pass through them, beating into the garamut of its own volition. I also noticed that although there was still a clear rhythm, it had changed entirely.

This seemed to continue for a long time but was probably less than a minute. As he stood there, the old man's body seemed to be vibrating and a low wailing sound was coming from his mouth. Suddenly, he cried out and fell to the floor, allowing the pole to fall with him. This was the first time the pole had been allowed to hit the ground since the start.

There was complete silence for about 10 seconds or so, and then the spell was broken as two women came forward and helped him to his feet, and everyone turned and walked away. I continued to stand there, desperately trying to understand what I had just seen and make sense of it.

In the villages of the Lower and Middle Ramu, people believe that, except for old age, the only way a person died would be if someone killed them or arranged their deaths, probably using a Sanguma: a magic man or woman.

Most groups of villages have a single Sanguma living within their midst. He or she is highly respected and feared and has strong magical powers. In particular, they have the ability to persuade. People believe so profoundly in these powers that, apparently, they often succumb.

So, if a Sanguma told you that you would set fire to your house at midday tomorrow and then lie on your bed and burn to death, you would probably do it without question.

Father George had tried to dispel this idea of death always being suspicious, and, in and around Giri Number 1, he had been partially successful. Many people began to accept that disease and illness can be a natural cause of death. However, most people are still very suspicious when a death occurs for no apparent reason. That is exactly what had happened in Giri Number 1. A man in his middle years had been found by his wife drowned on the bank of a stream. To anyone's knowledge, he had not been ill, nor were there signs of a struggle or any evidence to show how it could have happened. To most people, this was a classic case of death by witchcraft.

The belief was that a Sanguma would have been employed to kill him. He would have approached and told him that, at a specific time on a particular day, he would walk down to the river and drown. Such was his belief in the power of the Sanguma that he had done precisely what was instructed.

In many parts of New Guinea, 'Pay Back' is a way of life. If someone does something bad to a member of your family, murder, stealing or adultery, for example, then it is your duty or the duty of your kin to take revenge, payback. It might not happen immediately; it could be in five months, five years or even fifty years. It could even be carried out, not directly against the perpetrator of the crime, but against one of their children or even grandchildren.

It is a real nightmare for the police in larger towns investigating such crimes. Imagine solving a crime that's root was thirty years earlier and to someone completely different.

It is important to note that the Sanguma is rarely blamed; it is the person who employed them to do the deed who is guilty.

A few days later, I asked Joseph what the ceremony with the garamut meant. He told me that the people of Giri were asking their ancestors, through the rhythm of the drum, who had invoked the magic of the Sanguma to cause the man to drown. When the pole was apparently beating a new rhythm on its own through the hands of the elder, the ancestors were answering with the name of the killer. Sometime in the future, he or a member of his family would be killed in retribution.

Joseph was not comfortable telling me all this and refused to say who had been named or which village they came from. In fact, he told me, only a few people would have the knowledge to be able to understand the rhythm of the drum and the name of the guilty man. However, the dead man's family would be told and they would be expected to act.

One afternoon, I was alone with Venansius in his classroom we were practising a dance that the staff were going to do for the borders to entertain them on their first night back for the summer term. The other teachers had left, but apparently, I needed extra tuition. Venansius' was a straight talker and said,

"Richard, I have never met anyone as inept as you at putting one foot in front of the other and moving forward."

"I can walk and run perfectly normally thank you." I said defensively and I admit, rather haughtily, "my mum told me I began walking at a very early age and at school I was well known for my athletic prowess." (Complete fabrication)

"Well, it's a pity your mum didn't work on your development when you were a bit older, she should have taught you to dance."

In the end, he gave up and told me I could stand at the back, clap and sway a bit if I could manage that without falling over. Rather harsh, I felt.

I asked him if he knew about cargo cult. I'd been warned back in England that it could be a danger to foreigners in general and white people in particular.

"I've never experienced it in this part of New Guinea," he told me, "but it was a real problem when I worked in Port Moresby. You see, some people believe that spirits, our ancestors, control everything. The material things that come into the country for white people to have, were meant for them; the white people stole them. They were supposed to be for the native New Guineans. They actually believe that on the planes and boats that bring cargo, white people sneak into the holds and change the names and addresses, which is why some of them don't have to do work. They then sell the goods to New Guineans. When goods arrive and are collected, no money changes hands, yet if a black person wants something, they have to pay cash.

Did you know that, relatively recently, shells were the only form of currency here? The whole money system is wholly foreign to many people."

"So, if you believed in cargo cult, would that mean you think the clothes I am wearing really belong to you?" I asked.

He looked me up and down. "I Sincerely hope not," he replied.

Beating the Garamut

The Expert

Not the Expert

A man called Abraham wanted someone in his village killed; he suspected him of sleeping with his wife, so he employed a Sanguma from another village. However, he was not a real Sanguma but was clever enough to persuade people that he was. The Sanguma charged Abraham ten beetle nuts, ten yams and ten green bananas.

Once he had been paid, he instructed Abraham to go into the victim's hut when nobody was about and steal a loincloth or another piece of clothing that had been against his skin.

The pretend Sanguma took a piece of bamboo and blocked one end; he then captured a death adder, placed it in the bamboo with the item of clothing, and sealed it in. Using a stick, he beat the bamboo over and over for an hour. This was agonising for the snake, and it associated its torture with the smell of the cloth.

The pretend Sanguma then placed the bamboo next to a path he knew the victim would soon be walking. He attached some string to one of the seals so that a firm tug would dislodge it. As the victim passed the bamboo, he tugged the string. The snake slithered out, and there in front of it was the man with the smell that had caused its terrible ordeal. It attacked him and bit him over and over. He died in minutes.

Chapter 11   Recipe

As time went by, I became stronger both physically and mentally. I started walking further afield alone and relished the challenge of these jaunts.

I laughed at the memory of my first walk to Giri Number 2 when I had sworn that Giri Number 1 would be my furthest outing on foot.

As far as I could make out, when local people use the term bus (the bush), the meaning can include jungle, scrub, huge fields of long kunai grass and all manner of forests. In fact, it means anything other than villages. gardens, roads or anything else people have made.

My favourite places to walk in the 'bus' was the tropical rainforest or what I thought of as jungle. As you entered, the trees enveloped you and the air became so hot and sticky that sometimes it was difficult to breathe. The further you went, the more the canopy closed in. The occasional flash of lights from high up between the trees caught the birds, butterflies and other insects in a rainbow of different colours. It is not silent, and most of the noise is high above; a choir of hundreds of birds chattering their sweet melodies, with the bird of paradise as the star turn.

Down on the ground, the silence is only broken by the whine of mosquitoes and the scrunching of boots battling through the undergrowth. Sometimes, it is easy walking, but at other times, the shrubs, bushes, stunted trees and bamboo clumps make it impossible to go on.

In all my roaming, I always ensured I was within viewing distance of a path. These were often narrow and hard to see, some created by animal movement. Going into the bush unaided would have been a huge mistake, so I always carried a compass and, believe it or not, tied string to a tree or bush wherever paths crossed. I had a few scary moments but never got seriously lost.

I did not see many animals, although they must have been around. The largest were cassowaries, wild boar and tree kangaroos. I never saw a tree kangaroo, and research I have done since would suggest there were none in our area. Yet village people swore they had seen and hunted them and described them accurately. They are beautiful and I cannot think of a better word to describe them than cuddly.

The forest sometimes opened up to huge fields comprising mainly of kunai grass, green and yellow and sometimes as tall as a person.

Nearer the Ramu and its tributaries were groves of sago palms and forest, but the trees were not as tall and the undergrowth less dense. These areas regularly flooded during the wet season and were known as the sago swamps. They were really important for growing many of the commonly eaten foods, such as sago, yam, taro and sweet potato.

Sago was the staple diet in the Lower/Middle Ramu wetlands, certainly in the area around Giri, and was eaten with nearly every meal.

The basic ingredient is extracted from a sago palm, the most common locally being the metroxylong sagu. These palms grow to a great height, fifty feet or more, often in clusters. They can grow up to one and a half yards annually and were plentiful in the whole area.

The palm is cut down and split along its length. The bark must be removed so that the pith can be scraped out and shredded. The men do this first process. The women now take over and rinse and knead the pith. This process separates the starch from the fibrous residue.

This is very much a family affair. The men will be there while the women are doing their tasks and vice versa and the children help or play and are often given the job of searching through the waste fibrous material for bugs and fungi. These would be collected and roasted later. They would both make a tasty addition to the meal. The starch is then taken back to the village for the next stage.

Several different processes can follow, including making a kind of bread-like substance. In our area, however, the starch was mixed with boiling water and formed into a clear paste, and that is what was served. I did eat sago on many occasions, but I could not say that I liked the look or the taste, particularly as layers of dirt could be clearly seen within the food.

The process of making sago from one trunk would take the best part of a day and feed a family for several weeks.

Mosquitoes were a real problem. On one occasion, I was crossing a river on a single narrow tree trunk that passed as a bridge and I had to use both arms to help me keep my balance. I was wearing a T-shirt and when I reached the other side, I had so many mosquitoes on me that it was impossible to see any part of my arms.

On another occasion, I smelt burning and came out of a small forest to see a huge area of waist high kunai (sword grass) with a long line of flames blowing towards the east. At the edge of the field, people were ready with spears. As animals emerged from the grass to escape the fire, some were killed and carried back to the village. This was a form of hunting called 'burning the kunai.'

Weather conditions had to be just right for this method; there had to be a breeze but not too strong. They did not want the fire to get out of control and burn part of the forest.

Arengin was the furthest village that came under the responsibility of the mission. It was deep in the bush and a three to six hour walk from Giri, depending on the season and weather conditions.

It was very isolated, and apart from children who went to school, the majority of people only spoke the local Arengin language. Not many people wore anything but traditional dress, typically for men and women, was just a loincloth, waist high sari or grass skirt.

Those children of the village who went to school at Giri would set out from home Sunday at about midday, board for the week and Friday lunchtime they would head home. The average attendance was little more than one week in two. Father George had been to Arengin occasionally to say mass, but some people who lived deeper in the bush rather than in the main village had rarely or never seen a white person.

One Friday in June, I sent a message with Yuri Angaren, an Arengin boy in my class, to ask the elders if I could visit. I would be walking. On the next Monday, he told me they would be pleased to greet me on the coming Saturday and as it was such a long way, I should stay over and go back Sunday. Yuri and two other boys would stay at school and would accompany me. I was really pleased about that, as Father George had told me it would be easy to get lost.

We set off early in the morning and it was a wonderful trek. The paths were dry, which made things much easier, and in fact, we did it in well under four hours. We went through every kind of landscape.

The boys loved the fact that our roles were reversed; they were in charge and during the journey, they taught me a great deal about the plants, animals and life in Arengin.

The first visit was wonderful. I was treated like royalty. I don't think that people thought a foreigner would have either the inclination or the stamina to visit them. A lot of villagers turned out to greet me. It seemed to take an hour to shake everyone's hands. Some of them had never seen a white person before and, having looked me up and down, would touch my face, perhaps to check that I was real.

I was given the ultimate greeting: a feast. A pig was killed in my honour by the family of one of the pupils in my class, Michael. Pigs were normally reserved for Sing Sings and the like.

I sat around the fire with the family and other invited villagers, about thirty people in all. A huge wooden plate filled with sago was placed in front of us. On top of the sago were pieces of pork that had been baked in the embers of the fire, as well as yams and taros. On the command from the family elder, everyone began eating.

I had learnt my lesson and grabbed what I could and ate it as fast as possible. Michael laughed and said, "kaikai olsem manmeri I cam long hia." (You eat like the locals). Unfortunately for my family in England, it is a habit I maintain to this very day.

That evening, one of my pupils, Thomas, took me into the bush to a small community to meet his grandfather. His name was Aboua and he was very old by New Guinean standards. He looked quite frail and struggled to walk. He could not speak tok pisin and, unfortunately, Arengin had a completely different language from Giri. We sat on a log and chatted. Thomas acted as interpreter in a mixture of English and talk pisin.

He had already explained that he thought I would want to meet his grandfather as he had been a cannibal when he was a young man. He had been born in a tribe that lived in the foothills of the mountains. I asked him about it. Something had happened to cause Aboua to leave the tribe but he did not immediately say what. He made his way east and eventually came to Arengin, where he was accepted and allowed to stay. I asked him why he had to leave his village.

"When I was young, meat was easy to hunt. There was lots of game in the bush. Then white men came, looking for metals. They gave us guns in exchange for knowledge. Then, it became too easy to hunt, and soon the animals were gone. A hunting expedition had to spend days, sometimes weeks in the bush to get a reasonable haul and often came back empty handed.

One day, I was out on a hunt and accidentally shot and killed another man from the village. His family were upset and wanted revenge. They demanded that

I be killed, but the village elders met and decided it had been an accident and that I should not be killed but banished from the village instead."

I asked Aboua what he could remember about cannibalism and if he took part.

"If you killed a person of the same status during a battle, you could eat him. So, for instance, a warrior killing another warrior. If you killed a child or a woman, you could not eat their flesh."

He looked thoughtful and I wondered if he was telling me things he had been part of or things that he had known to happen.

"You did not just grab an arm and eat," he said and then laughed, which led to a coughing fit. "The meat was shared with everyone who had fought in the battle and their families. It meant each person only getting a small piece. It was all a ritual, really."

I asked him how he prepared a person for eating.

"First, you tie the body to a pole and turn it slowly over the fire; this burns the body hair off the carcass. A hole as deep as a man must be dug and huge fires made. Large flat stones are put on the fires until they are red hot and some are used to line the bottom of the hole. On top of these are placed vegetables: yams, taros, sweet potatoes and green bananas. Another layer of hot stones is laid and then the body. This is covered by yet another layer of hot stones then vegetables and then hot stones.

By now, there is about this much of the hole remaining." He pointed to the distance from his knees to the ground. "This is filled in with earth and trodden down. The position of the underground oven is marked by sticks. These are shaped, and, sometimes, painted in the victim's blood. The body is left for three full days to cook slowly. It is then dug up and eaten."

"What does it taste like?" I asked.

"It tastes a bit like pork but not as sweet." he told me. "The whole process is showing victory over your enemies but also respect for the victim."

I asked him if he regretted leaving his old village.

"It turned out to be a good thing. My old village was always fighting with others and many people were killed. It is different here.

The Arengin villagers never really get on with the people of Tebran. The two villages are still not friendly and have fought in the past. Nobody really remembers why. Now the children go to school together, and everything is changing."

Thomas nodded, "I am good friends with Peter from Tebran; I sit next to him in your class."

I wanted to ask more but Aboua was tired and needed to rest.

"Come again, young man," he said. "I have many more stories I can tell you."

Sadly, it was not to be. A few weeks later, Thomas brought the news that his grandfather had died in his sleep.

Serving the saksak (sago) for the evening meal

A Field of Kunai
Burning the Kunai
A young wild boar has been killed and being taken
back to the village

Bupa Lived with his parents in the village of Twarie, on the banks of the Sepik River. Bupa was twelve years old. Bupa Had a cousin, Guu who was thirteen years old and lived in a nearby village. This village had an outbreak of a disease and both Guu's parents died. Bupa's parents allowed Guu to come and live with them.

Bupa was very unhappy and jealous about this and did all he could to make Guu's life difficult.

One day when his parents were out at their garden, he took some of his father's betel nuts and hid them in Guu's bedding. When they returned, he told them he had seen Guu steal the betel nuts.

Bupa's father searched Guu's bedding and found the betel nuts. He was furious. He beat Guu with a stick. Another time Bupa told his father that Guu was stealing food and was keeping it under a log in the bush. Bupa's father found the food that Bupa had planted, beat Guu and gave him no food for two days.

Another time Bupa took his father's spear and killed his favourite dog. He then put spots of blood on Guu's clothes.

His father was iridescent with rage and grief. He beat Guu so badly that he nearly died, didn't feed him for two days and made him sleep under the hut with the pigs for a week.

Bupa's mother was suspicious, she could not understand why Guu was being so bad. He was a good boy when he lived with his own parents. She kept an eye on the two children and one day she saw Bupa take one of his father's Sing Sing headdresses and break it up, he then placed a small feather from the headdress in Guu's bed.

116

She told her husband. He was very upset and made Bupa admit to all the things that Guu had been blamed for.

He thought about what he should do for days and finally decided he could not live with his son any longer. He took him deep into the bush and told him he would kill him if he ever returned to the village. Bupa cried and begged his father for forgiveness, but his father walked away.

When he told his wife what he had done, she screamed with anguish and ran into the bush to find her son. Neither of them was ever seen again.

Chapter 12   Harold

Bonnie and Hans shared a small hut near Father Georges' house. They cooked, cleaned, and did most of the minor maintenance around the station and any other tasks the father gave them.

Bonnie had a friend called Harold, who looked like an old man but was probably in his forties. As far as I could tell, he lived in a village a long way upstream of the Ramu River, perhaps in the foothills of the mountains.

Every year, he walked from his home to Bogia, where he had a nephew. He would stay there for three or four days and then walk back. He was on his way home now.

He stayed in various villages on the way, including Giri. He would arrive in the afternoon and leave the following morning. He always had a story or two to tell and had become an institution.   Father George tolerated him, fed him and let him stay with Hans and Bonnie in their hut.

Bonnie invited me to spend an hour or two with them in the evening. So, we sat in my classroom, ate betel nuts and smoked while Harold told us in tok pisin about the time an Australian patrol officer came to his village and appointed a police officer.

The concept of a police officer upholding the law was alien to his people and, in fact, to most New Guineans who lived in villages. Sometimes people did bad things but it was sorted out as a community and the ultimate punishment was to be told to leave the village. That was huge. It seemed to be the equivalent of losing your citizenship. You were a refugee for life. He couldn't remember it ever happening in his lifetime.

There were no volunteers for the job, and in the end, the patrol officer appointed a young man named Ahma, whose father was a village elder. He was not really a good choice as he had a reputation for being rather devious and unkind. He was neither popular nor, more importantly, was he respected.

He was given a badge to wear, a hat and a letter of appointment, which he couldn't read. Apparently, so he said, the letter contained a list of crimes he could deal with and the punishments he could inflict. There were two main ones. The first was arresting and removing the right to move around; the perpetrator was required to stay in their home and not go out or meet anyone for up to two weeks. The second was issuing a fine.

All went well for a few months until Ahma started to flex his police muscles. It started with him making up crimes and picking on weaker members of the community.

These included:

>   starting a cooking fire at the wrong time
>   allowing smoke to blow in the wrong direction
>   women talking too loudly
>   children urinating in public places

None of these things were particularly unusual, nor did anyone see them as a problem.

These crimes and many others were punished with fines of tobacco, beetle nuts, headdresses, food and sometimes incarceration. At one time, half the village seemed to be confined in their huts. His favourite punishment was to make people work for him, tend his garden, clean and cook. As time went on, he made more and more demands on the people of the village.

If anyone refused, he would say that he would have to go and fetch the patrol officer, who was only a few hours away. When he arrived, he would beat the criminals with his stick and take them to Port Moresby, where they would be thrown into an underground dungeon and kept there for years. People were genuinely frightened of Ahma and the power he wielded.

Well, tyrants tend to come to a sticky end.

Turee was a quiet and well respected young man who lived in the village. He was known for his great strength, his common sense and his beautiful wife.

Police Officer Ahma would not normally take on someone as influential and strong as Turee but he was besotted with his wife. His jealousy and desire for her were overwhelming. He lay in bed at night thinking about her and how wonderful it would be if she were with him. He couldn't understand why Turee should be so lucky, after all, he didn't deserve her.

'She should be with me.' He thought. 'She probably secretly desires me because of my good looks and status, and after all, I am a police officer, a very important man, without a doubt, the most important man in the village.'

One evening, he went to see Turee, who was sitting outside his house. He told him that the law says Turee must allow Ahma to sleep with his wife for one night every week. Turee chewed his beetle nut reflectively and then spat the red juice over Ahma's foot.

Ahma went mad, shouting and ranting. Soon, everyone in the village had come to see what was happening. Ahma put his foot on a log and demanded that Turee lick the juice off his foot or he would arrest him.

A sigh of disappointment came from the crowd as Turee bent down compliantly. However, instead of licking his foot as Ahma was expecting, Turee took his big toe into his mouth and bit with all his might.

Ahma screamed with pain, and the villagers cheered and shouted their appreciation. Once free, he limped back to his hut, shouting abuse and threats, blood pouring from what was left of his toe.

The following morning, Ahma was gone; there was no sign of him anywhere. Some of the villagers were worried that he had gone to get the patrol officer. Turee did not seem concerned in the slightest and told them not to worry.

Harold sat there smiling at the memory. I asked him where he thought Ahma had gone. He gazed at me in a strange way.

"I don't really know," he said and looked away. The penny dropped and I didn't ask anything more; I didn't want him to confirm my suspicions.

The following morning, we saw Harold off, and I gave him a packet of Australian cigarettes, a real luxury, and a tin of fish. I told him it was a thank you for telling us such a great story.

Then, I made a major error of judgement.

"Where is your home from here, Harold?" I asked, "I mean, how far away is it?"

Out of the corner of my eye, I saw Hans look shocked and quietly sneak away around the corner of the building. Bonnie put his head in his hands and muttered a noise that sounded like a groan.

Harold seemed to puff up his chest and thought for a moment; he then pointed to the southwest and said,

"i go, (you go) i go, i go, i go, i go, i go, i go, i go, i go, i go, i go, i go, i go, i go, i go, i go, i go, i go, i go."

Every i go was accompanied by a hand movement to show any directional change in the route, including uphill or downhill.

"i go, i go, i go, i go, i go, i go, i go, i go, i go, i go, i go, i go, i go, i go, i go, i go, i go, i go."

And so it went on and on and on. For a full twenty minutes, no exaggeration; **twenty minutes.** He mapped out his entire journey for me. Thank goodness he hadn't come from Port Moresby; I would still be there.

Just as I was seriously considering ending my own life or, better still, his, he stopped. I guess we had reached his home. He nodded and went on his way, and I never saw him again.

Later, Bonnie told me that many of the older villagers used this method to give directions but of course, it would almost always be somewhere local, a good sago clump, for instance. I asked Bonnie if he thought the directions that Harold had given me were accurate (quite a difficult thing to do in tok pisin). He thought about this for several minutes.

"It is possible, but I don't think so," he replied, "I think he just enjoyed seeing you suffer."

In the village of Sambu lived a widow called Akiah. Her husband had died and some of the villagers decided she must have caused his death. He had fallen from a tall Cliff and broken his neck on the rocks below. She was not there at the time of death but it was thought she had employed a Sanguma to kill him.

People did not want to go near her, so she lived a lonely life. She spent most of her time in her small hut, only going out to collect vegetables from her garden, firewood from the forest and water from the river.

One day she took her bamboo to the river to collect some water and there, in the stream, she saw an object that had light shining from it. She waded in and looked closely and realised it was the moon. The only thing she could think of was that it must have fallen out of the sky.

She ran back to her hut and fetched an old shirt that had belonged to her husband. She wrapped the moon in the shirt and, making sure nobody was watching, took it to her hut. She decided it would be very useful; she could work at night instead of during the day and she would not have to put up with the hostile stares and horrible remarks from her neighbours.

When the sun went down that night, the villagers couldn't understand why there was no moon, it was pitch dark. They became frightened and thought that their ancestors must be punishing them and wondered what they had done wrong.

A few nights later, a girl called Mary was on her veranda when she saw a slight glow in the distance. She told her mother, father, and brother but none of them could make out what it was.

They went from hut to hut, gathering all the villagers and crept quietly towards the light. When they got there, they saw Akiah tidying her garden and there on the ground, was the moon, partly wrapped in the shirt.

They were furious and demanded to know why she had the moon. She told them the story. They said she was selfish and mean for not telling them and sharing.

One of the young men, who was known for his strong arms, pushed her to the ground and then picked up the moon and threw it back up into the sky where it has stayed ever since.

Sadly, he forgot to remove the shirt, so when we can see only part of the moon, it is because the shirt has slipped and is covering the rest.

Chapter 13   The Beating

It seems a strange thing to say but I was born and brought up in the poor part of Woking. Yes, I know, I know; Woking - poor part - can't be true. But it is true, a section of housing down by the Basingstoke Canal, Vale Farm Road and Wilbury Road. In the fifties and sixties, life was tough there. Now, I will be the first person to admit that it wasn't Hackney's murder mile or Hell's Kitchen, New York, but all the same, you had to be careful what you did and said; there were some hard men and women living there.

I managed to avoid trouble very successfully. I was respectful to everyone, never took sides and could run fast. So, my first experience of real violence came as a shock.

I was eleven and it was my first day at Goldsworth Secondary School for Boys. When the newbies arrived, gangs of older pupils were waiting. They grabbed the new kids, dragged them into the toilets, forced their heads down the pan, and pulled the chain. Afterwards, they beat them up for good measure using their fists and boots. And when you thought it was over, another group would grab you and do the same again. That was scary, and a lot of blood flowed that day.

Now you might ask, where were all the teachers while this was going on? Should they not have been out there protecting their young charges?

Oh, they were there all right, drinking their mugs of coffee and smoking their Marlboroughs whilst watching and laughing. Perhaps they were just there to make sure nobody died. Or perhaps it was just for their own entertainment.

Over the next seven years, I, like everyone else, had the odd playground punch up but nothing nasty. My next experience of actual violence didn't happen until 1969.

One Tuesday in May, I was clearing up my classroom at the end of the school day when two young men, who looked to be in their twenties, came to the window and asked if they could speak to me. They said they were from a village called Amarn, approximately a three hour trek from Giri. It was not part of our mission area but was near the Ramu River, downstream from Giri number 2.

They explained that the village elders wanted to invite me to a celebration Sing Sing on Saturday. They wanted me to be the guest of honour, and I could stay over and return on Sunday. They told me that a young man called Rufus, who lived in Giri number 2, knew Amarn and I should ask him to be my guide.

I had never heard of Amarn but felt quite chuffed and honoured to be asked. I wondered how they had heard about me.

That evening, I wandered down to Giri Number 2 and asked to speak to Rufus. When he arrived, I didn't recognise him and realised I had never met him before. He was a small man, probably in his late twenties. He looked a little overweight, and his face seemed to have a permanent smirk. He was the kind of person that, I felt, would be difficult to like.

I asked him if he would be my guide, but he did not seem overly keen, and in the end, I had to offer him a dollar and the usual sheets of newspaper before he would agree.

The following Saturday afternoon, we set off, and when we reached Amarn, it was early evening, and a boy was waiting for us on the road. However, instead of leading us into the village, he turned off and took us to a house on its own, a hundred yards into the bush. The boy left us there, telling us his uncle would come and greet us soon.

It occurred to me that when we had passed the village, I had not noticed the usual noise and activity that accompanied the preparation for a Sing Sing. I began to feel a little concerned, especially as Rufus was looking and acting in a very agitated manner.

Suddenly, four men, including the two who had invited me the previous Tuesday, came out of the bush. Rufus saw them and, with a cry of fear, ran up the steps into the house. It was obvious that something was happening that I knew nothing about. I tried to get in front of them and talk to them but they easily pushed me out of the way and followed Rufus.

I quickly got up and chased them up the steps onto the veranda. It was gloomy inside but I could just make out Rufus cowering on the floor, using his arms to try and protect his head. They had surrounded him and were punching and kicking his body and face. From the force and violence they were meting out, I knew this was serious, and I had to stop them.

I screamed for them to stop, but it had no effect. I ran in and shouted as loudly as I could that they should leave him alone and tried to pull them away; they didn't even look up. All I could do was to try and stop them by getting between them and Rufus and try and grab hold of their arms.

I was getting very scared and panicky and I honestly believe they were going to kill him if I couldn't find a way to stop them.

Suddenly, a horrible pain seared through the left side of my face. I staggered across the room and crashed into the flimsy wall of the Hut. I was vaguely aware that they had stopped hitting Rufus and were staring towards me. At that moment, the wall gave way and I fell out of the hut and onto the ground.

I sat up rather groggily and watched as the four men ran out of the house and into the bush. I felt rather sick and the side of my head hurt but I also felt sure I was not badly damaged. I could hear Rufus crying.

I don't think what had happened to me was deliberate, a stray punch, most probably. The truth is however, it might have saved Rufus' life! I realised he was now quiet and I quickly went to him. He was barely conscious.

At that moment, people from the village arrived; I guess they had been alerted by the noise. They fetched water and bathed Rufus' wounds. A village elder asked me what had happened. After I explained, he told me there was no celebration or Sing Sing that weekend and that he had never heard of me. He said we should stay in the hut overnight and they would bring us food. He would arrange for some men to stay nearby to ensure our safety and he would come and see us in the morning.

I think he was worried about the repercussions for his village. After all, his own people had lied to a teacher from a catholic mission in order to lure their victim and then injured them both.

I assured him I did not blame him or anyone else apart from the four assailants.

I realised I had been duped. The attackers had obviously used me to bring Rufus to them. I wondered what he had done, and I guessed it would be to do with a woman, perhaps him seducing someone's daughter, wife or sister. Or perhaps he had stolen something valuable. I decided not to ask. It was possible he deserved his beating, although, I shuddered to think where it might have led had I not ended up crashing out of the house onto the ground.

In the morning, Rufus was well enough to walk, although it would be a long, slow journey home. I think he was concussed.

I was still furious, not because of the headache I was still suffering from, due to the blow and the fall, nor for what they had done to Rufus. It was really because they had fooled me, played on my naiveté. And I had been stupid enough and vain enough to fall for it.

When the village elder came to see us off, he told me they knew who the men were, but they had not returned overnight and were hiding in the bush. I told them that I hoped he would ensure they were suitably punished for their actions.

Yet another error of judgement on my part.

When I arrived back in Giri, Father George looked at the bruise on my face but didn't comment. He didn't ask about my trip, and I didn't feel the need to tell him what had happened. I talked to the other teachers about it that evening hoping for some sympathy and a recognition that perhaps I had been just a little brave. I should have known better; to a man, they found it hilarious, and Leo laughed so much that he fell off his chair. They actually asked me if I'd reenact the part where I fell through the wall. Unbelievably, Venansius had the nerve to make up a song on the spot and sang it to the accompaniment of his guitar.

Oh, Richard went to wandering along a jungle path
heading for a village where he thought he'd have a laugh
he was pleased to be so popular and loved throughout the place
but when he arrived to earn their praise, they punched him in the face

Ho Ho Ho, I thought.

During the evening, more verses were added by the other teachers, but fortunately, I managed to erase them from my memory.

It was just what I needed, to be brought down to earth, and soon I was laughing and singing along with them.

The next day I walked to Giri Number 2, and checked on Rufus, and found he was recovering well. I gave him his payment and a few tins of fish as a bonus, and he seemed happy with that.

The following Wednesday, I had just started my afternoon lessons when Father George and Venansius entered my classroom. They both looked rather shaken. Father told me I needed to accompany him to his house. Meanwhile, Venansius would keep an eye on my class as well as teach his own. I quickly set them some work.

When we arrived, there was the elder from Amarn standing with five others and, sitting on the ground,

130

were the four attackers. I gasped when I saw them and came close to being sick.

Their hands were tied in front of them. They had bruising and burns on their bodies, but it was their faces that actually shocked me to tears. They had literally been beaten to a pulp; it was awful. I couldn't speak I was so upset.

There was obviously an expectation that I should be pleased and grateful. I looked at Father George and he gave me a slight nod of the head. I said nothing, turned and walked back to my classroom and left him to do whatever he felt necessary.

I was upset for days knowing that the punishment had been at my behest. Finally, John got fed up with me moping about, and gave me the betel nut treatment. Then Venansius just said.

"Richard, you weren't to know what they would do. Next time, you will, and you'll be more careful what you say. There's an end to it."

I loved those two young men. Each, in their own way, were the kindest and wisest people I've ever met.

Hundreds of years ago, in the Lower Ramu, perhaps ten miles from the river, there were a group of villages. The people who lived in them were known as the Ruan. They were very warlike and nearly all the communities around them had been attacked in the past, driven away and their villages destroyed by fire. The Ruan did not take prisoners but tortured and killed any men they captured and took some of the women as slaves.

Some of the Ruan did not like this aggressive way of living and said it was wrong. But they were the minority and so nothing changed.

Over a period of weeks, the Ruan were aware of a strange phenomenon. Every so often, the ground would shake for a few seconds, and, as time went on, the shaking became more pronounced.

Then, one night, they were woken by a terrible rumbling noise. The ground began to shake in a way it never had before, and some huts collapsed. Slowly, the sky turned as red as blood and the people were very frightened and ran into the bush. The people cried out to their ancestors to forgive them as they believed they must have done something wrong to make them want to punish the people.

The movement and sound lasted for hours and gradually, the redness in the sky darkened and faded into black.

When morning came, the shaking had stopped but the sun didn't rise; the darkness remained and it was many days before normality returned. When they went back to their villages, there was a great deal of damage; many houses had collapsed and everything was covered with thick black dust.

Those villages who had wanted a less aggressive way of life blamed the others and said the ancestors and the sun and moon had punished the Ruan people for their violent crimes. This time they won the day and the Ruan decided to change. The first thing they did was to tell the slaves they had taken, that they could leave if they wished. Over the next few weeks, there was more ground shaking and the decision was taken to leave the area. The night before they went, they held a Sing Sing to honour their ancestors and the sun and the moon and to ask for forgiveness. In the morning, they left and were never heard of again.

Manam Island is an active volcano island not far off the coast to the east of the Lower Ramu Region. It last erupted in 2022. I wonder if the story, if it is based on real happenings, is describing Manam erupting in the past and the tremors that accompanied it. There is no way to date this story, so it is impossible to verify.

Chapter 14   The Boxer

During the Easter holiday, Father George sent Bonnie to find me and bring me to his house. He was sitting on his veranda and told me that he had received a letter from mission headquarters saying that one of the VSO's directors, Mr Carey, was in New Guinea and wanted to meet the volunteers. A helicopter would be landing in two days to take me to Madang. It would also be an opportunity to catch up with all the other volunteers in the district and that I would be returned three days later. I had met Mr Carey before, in London's Hanover Square.

The second round of my application for VSO had been an interview with him and he was fearsome. The first words he said to me were not, sit down or how are you? No as I walked through the door,

"Mr Masters, I see you obtained nine O levels, but all with low grades, and your school does not expect you to pass any A levels. You do understand that two A level passes is a minimum requirement for working abroad with VSO."

I actually thought about walking out there and then. For an hour, he plied me with all kinds of questions about my school, my home life, ambitions, hopes and fears.

Looking back now, I realise he was bearing my soul, finding the real me, checking that I could and would cope with isolation, loneliness, different cultures, and the challenge of being self-sufficient. Finally, he said,

"Right Mr Masters, we are nearly finished. As you know, if you are selected, we will choose the country where we feel your skills would be most useful, but you gave your preference as Papua New Guinea, why?"

I answered truthfully, "it was the only country on the list I had never heard of."

A hint of a smile appeared on his face. It may be complete nonsense, but I have a feeling that the answer I gave may have swung the outcome in my favour.

Apparently, less than 2% of volunteers return home before their time is up, such as the testament to Mr Carey and his team.

I was not hopeful, and when, three weeks later, the letter came telling me I had been accepted, I was ecstatic and not a little nervous. Going to New Guinea for a year had suddenly become a reality.

Back at school, I went to see my headteacher and asked him about what Mr Carey had said about A level results. Strangely he got out of his seat, went over to the door, and checked that no one was lurking outside, listening.

"Just between you and me," he said, "you will be only days away from leaving by the time the results come out. There is no way they can pull you out that late. Just do your best. Oh, and by the way, well done; I'm really proud of you."

It is one of the few times I can remember a teacher saying something positive and encouraging to me; I had to hold back tears.

I regret to say that I did indeed fail all three of my A levels: Physics, Maths and even Geology, although I got an A for the practical, and it has been a great love of mine ever since. I could not bring myself to tell my mum and dad the truth, so I lied to them and said that I had passed all three. Two years on, that lie was to have serious repercussions.

The helicopter arrived and landed on the football pitch. I had mentioned to a few people in the village that if they came to the mission, they would see something special. Their reactions were varied. A few ran into the bush in fear, some stood open-mouthed, but others, had heard of such things and were smiling and clapping. I asked the pilot if he would let Joseph and Abi aboard just to see inside but he was anxious to get going and said no. He probably got asked that sort of thing all the time.

Mr Carey was on board as well as the other two volunteers who had been stationed in the interior. On the journey, Mr Carey asked us about our experiences so far. He wanted to know how we were getting on, any problems we had had and if there were any changes that could be made to the training we were given before leaving England. I didn't mention the issues I'd had in the first few months, but I had a feeling that he knew about them. The other two were very positive about their experience so far and made it sound as if it had all been plain sailing and relatively mundane. I wondered if they had really experienced the same ups and downs that I had.

About six weeks before we all left for our different destinations, a number of volunteers had met at the University of Birmingham for a week's induction.

The group comprised of eighty young people, some the same age as me, others had just graduated from university. We were going to many different places in the world, and, in small groups, we learned about health issues, including malaria, homesickness, the effects of heat and many other things.

There were about ten of us going to Papua New Guinea, and we were told a lot about the history, geography and culture. We were shown how Pidgin English worked and encouraged to learn and practise it. I was a poor student and did not take advantage of the knowledge available. However, the teaching tips and techniques I did make note of.

As we approached Madang, I asked Mr Carey if the induction would have worked better if done in countries, so all the volunteers from each target country would be together. He said they had thought about doing it that way but decided against it. He didn't explain why.

We stayed in a hostel and met every day in a large gymnasium. They had devised lots of activities for us, some were social events, but they also took the opportunity to check our physical health and well-being. We were all examined by a doctor and interviewed by what now would be described as a counsellor.

It occurred to me that seven months ago, I had been seriously ill, suffering from depression. Now, I could not have been happier. I was fit, healthy and handsome. (OK maybe tone down on the handsome a bit) Undoubtedly, I was enjoying my life.

We were each given ten dollars and when we had free time, I would go into the centre of Madang and just wander around. There were cafes, restaurants and shops of all kinds but the people running them were all white or of Asian appearance. I discovered the only jobs done by native New Guineans were done behind the scenes; cleaning, washing up and other menial jobs. I found that strange as it was their country.

I met Father Ignatius, who was visiting from Port Moresby. It turned out he had a cousin in Guilford whom he had visited. She lived only a few streets away from my Auntie Win. We sat down one morning for a coffee and a chat.

Ignatius had travelled extensively in New Guinea and had a great interest in non-indigenous people's effect on the lives of ordinary local people, especially those in villages. He told me that during the war, the Japanese have been ruthless at times, stripping communities of food and resources, leading to some people dying of starvation. Villagers were made to work in forced labour camps and were killed if they showed any sign of disobedience. And yet, he regularly met people who preferred the Japanese to other outsiders whom they found devious and likely to let them down. With the Japanese, you knew where you were, is what they said.

In the war years, Australian and American soldiers who had been wounded were regularly rescued by local people, looked after, and returned to their armies. This took considerable time, effort and bravery. The Japanese would have certainly executed both the soldiers and their rescuers if they had been caught.

There was one thing that most of the people he talked to agreed on. They would like all the people from outside to leave and let them run their own country. The bottom line was that the outsiders were selfish and would ruin their lands. There was a real irony in this as fifty years on, independence has happened and it is the government that is failing to protect its people from outsiders.

The gym had a boxing ring, and, on the last evening, one of the organisers suggested we paired up and had some contests. I would not say I liked the idea at all; I had never really been keen on fighting and had always avoided confrontation where possible. However, everybody else seemed to think it was a great idea, or pretended to, so I really felt I had to go for it. I decided the best thing to do was to find someone who looked as if I had a chance of beating, or at least, wouldn't hurt me too much. I considered one of the girls, but the truth is they all look terribly strong and scary.

Dave, however, seemed a perfect choice. He was a bit of a loner, rarely talked to anyone and when he did it tended to be monosyllabic. I had said hi to him at breakfast that morning, and I swear he growled at me. He was skinny, quite short and, most importantly, did not seem to be the sharpest pencil in the pot.

"Fancy taking me on Dave?" I said in a cocky sort of voice.

"Grrr," he said, which I guess meant yes.

Our turn came, and into the ring we went. The bell rang for the first round and I danced around for a minute or two, quite impressively I felt, every bit the sportsman. Finely toned muscles rippling in the harsh light, skinny legs elegantly gliding around the ring like a ballroom dancer. I certainly hoped some of the young women were watching.

He didn't really move very much, just turned so he was always facing me, his arms dangling down by his sides. It was like he either did not know how to defend himself or just couldn't be bothered.

'What an idiot,' I thought to myself.

I went in close and punched him in the midriff, no reaction. I did the same again, only harder. Strange, he still didn't react. I couldn't understand why he hadn't fallen to the ground, submitted and begged for mercy. I weaved in again, and this time went for his face; he swayed back, and the blow only glanced him across the forehead. 'That's it,' I thought angrily, 'enough pussyfooting, I'm going to finish this.'

I checked that the audience was watching attentively, then stepped in for the killer blow. And then, nothing.

When I came to, I was lying on my back on a massage table. I had a terrible pain around the chin area and a headache. Sitting next to me was Dave.

"Hello," he said, "sorry about that, I hope it isn't too painful. It was an uppercut and, well, I caught you on the chin a bit harder than I meant to."

I nodded feebly and tried to smile. Smiling hurt!

"Look, don't feel bad. Everyone makes the same mistake when they meet me for the first time, they always think I'm weedy and thick. I'm not an extrovert and I don't particularly enjoy blowing my own trumpet, but the truth is last year I got to the finals of the junior Midlands featherweight ABA championship. The year before that, I actually won my age category. I also got four As at A level and have a place at Cambridge University when I get back.

Look, tell you what, give it an hour, then go back in the ring; everybody will think you're dead brave. Offer the tall geezer over there a fight, he's even worse than you are. I think his name is Henry."

I went three rounds with Henry, and I don't think either of us landed a serious punch. Those watching quickly became bored silly and moved away. Even the referee went and sat down in one of the corners and smoked his pipe.

I spent the rest of the evening happily chatting with Henry and Dave while others tried to punch the lights out of each other. At one point, I asked Dave if there was any chance of me being a decent boxer.

"Well, let me think," he said thoughtfully, "ah yes, if you actually concentrated on the fight rather than worrying about what impression you were making on the young ladies watching, that might help."

I sat there, stunned for a few moments, and then we all burst out laughing. I learned a lot that day.

Not everyone has been knocked out by a Cambridge University ABA boxing champion, in Papua New Guinea.

When I was growing up, I was often compared to my cousin Ian who lived in Guildford. He was a couple of years older than me and he was good at everything he did. My mum was always saying Ian this and Ian that, why can't you be like Ian, Ian came top of his class at school, why can't you do the same? I should have hated him but he was actually a really nice chap so I forgave him for being clever and for being such a goody goody.

About ten years after leaving Papua New Guinea he visited my wife and me in London. I hadn't seen him for many years. He said he enjoyed squash and asked if I played. I have always had a mischievous streak and occasionally had been known to tell a harmless lie. Anyway, for some reason, beyond my comprehension, I told him I was New Guinea Squash Open champion. This, despite having never actually played the game in my life. He was really impressed and I could see his respect for me had risen dramatically. At last, I was better than him at something, sort of.

After he'd gone, I told my wife, thinking she would laugh and admire my fun nature. Actually, she just gave me that look!

Some months later, my wife and I visited Ian at his home in Kent and, after a fine lunch, he announced that he had booked a squash court for three o-clock and was really looking forward to playing against an open champion.

Fortunately, I could say that I had no kit, but apparently, he had told my wife some days earlier of his plans and the treacherous woman had brought all that was needed; she'd even borrowed a racket for me. I tried to stare her down, but she had a hand over her face to hide the fact she was killing herself laughing.

142

We arrived at the court and Ian apologised in advance. He said he probably would not be able to give me much of a game, although he had won his club championship a few months earlier.

You can imagine what happened; he stood in the middle of the court while I was run ragged. He walloped and embarrassed me and showed no mercy whatsoever.

Afterwards, I crawled off the court with a bright red face and sweat pouring off me. When I had recovered somewhat, I expected, at the very least, some difficult questions, but he never said a word about it, which actually made it even worse. I suppose he didn't really need to. I do wonder if he suspected I was lying all along.

Back in the car, my wife said she was very sorry. Although, I have to say she didn't look terribly distressed.

Chapter 15   Jim

At the beginning of July, I came to a decision. I went to see Father George and told him that I did not want to leave in August as planned; I would like to stay on.

One of the reasons was that I felt my first months had been both awful and wasted, and in my mind, I had only really started being a volunteer of any use at Christmas. I wanted to do at least a full year if not longer.

He told me that a new volunteer was arriving, and it would be unfair not to give him a class of his own. After my experience when I started, I understood that but I had a plan which I outlined to him.

The idea would be to stay in Giri for a couple of weeks to help the new volunteer settle in and then move to Arengin. There, I would set up a school for children who were too young to do the long journey to Giri and back every week. I was also keen to help older people learn Pidgin English or even English.

Father George mulled over the idea for a few days and finally agreed. He also said I must be crazy to want to do this.

I wrote to VSO and explained what I intended to do, and some weeks later, I was summoned to Bogia to meet Father Delany, who had been sent from Alexishafen. He told me that there were two significant problems.

Firstly, VSO got a half price concession from the airline BOAC. This meant that if I went ahead, the return ticket money would be put in the trust of the mission headquarters, and they would organise my travel when the time came, but only to the amount that VSO had given. It would be a great deal less than the full cost of a flight home to the UK.

Secondly, although the mission would continue looking after my welfare to an extent, it would not be to the same level that VSO offered. Basically, I would no longer be being supported by VSO. I agreed to this and the deal was done.

When I was three years old, I remember seeing my two oldest brothers fighting at the top of the stairs at our home. Gordon, the eldest, pushed Peter down the stairs. Other than that, I have no other memory of Gordon as he emigrated to New Zealand a few weeks later, and I had not seen him since. He had made a good life for himself and was now married with three children.

The money from VSO would get me to Auckland, where he lived, and I didn't really want to think any further than that.

In August, Jim, the new volunteer, arrived in Giri. He seemed a thoroughly nice person and, as with me when I arrived, he was eighteen, straight out of school, and pretty nervous.

We spent a few days going over school stuff and meeting some of the local children in my class that he would take over. I also made sure he knew how the generator worked.

I'm ashamed to say that I decided to play a joke on him with Joseph's help.

He had been there about a week when I told him a family in the village had invited him for a traditional

New Guinea meal, which was a great honour. That evening we wandered down to Giri Number 1 and found Joseph's family and a few others sitting around the cooking fire. Once I had introduced everyone, Abi spooned out the food. Everybody was given a normal portion of sago and some pieces of meat. However, Jim had a far bigger plate and, as the special guest, at least twice the amount of food.

Jim looked at his meal with horror. He took a spoonful of the sago, which was even dirtier than usual, swallowed, and then ate a piece of meat. He smiled and nodded appreciatively in the direction of Abi and Joseph and then turned to me and whispered.

"Do I have to eat it all? It's an awful lot."

I Looked solemn, "it would be a great insult if you didn't finish it. They would be very upset and might even put an evil spell on you, which would make you very ill. You certainly wouldn't be welcome in the village again. Anyway, it's not too bad, and the roast rat is particularly well cooked and tasty."

He went as white as a sheet, leapt up and ran into the nearby bush. We could all hear him retching. I have to say I felt terrible; I went to find him and told him it was a joke and that he didn't have to eat it, and that the meat wasn't rat. This was not actually true, but it seemed a good idea not to tell him that at the time. Maybe in a few days or even years. Actually, he may be reading it for the first time in this book.

Walking back to the mission, I apologised and promised there would be no more jolly japes.

I don't think Joseph and Abi had a clue as to what had happened, but they were quite happy to share out and eat what Jim had left.

The following week, the term started, Jim began his teaching career, and I set off for Arengin.

Jim sharing a joke with the staff in Giri
Leo far right, John Pious far left

Jim and Venansius on a trek in the wet season

A long time ago, there was only one man. The rains came, causing great flooding, and all that was left that could be seen were the tops of mounds and hills surrounded by water.

The man had a dream and was told what he must do. He was to build a simple canoe, and taking with him a sharpened stick, he was to paddle to each island and pierce the ground. Each time he did this, two animals came out of the hole. A male and a female of the same species. On the tallest hill, he pierced the ground, and a woman appeared from the spot.

The flood subsided and the animals went into the bush but the woman stayed with him and they had many children.

If there had been more mounds and hills, there would have been other species that are unknown to us.

A Giri man told me this ancient tale after hearing the story of Noah's Ark in church. I asked him if this was something he had heard in church or had it originally come from a visitor. He was absolutely positive it was a very old traditional tale and came from long before white people first came to the area.

Chapter 16   Arengin

A young man named Albert arrived from Arengin to help me move my things. He proudly explained that he was named after a 'bikpela man belong inglen' (an important man from England). There wasn't too much to carry; I had borrowed an old, battered suitcase from Venansius and managed to cram everything in.

The journey took four and a half hours, and we took turns to do the carrying. Albert spoke good Pidgin English, and on the way, he told me he had gone to Bogia for work, and the church mission there had employed him to do odd jobs. He had stayed for over two years.

He had learnt a lot about gardening and, sometime in the future, he would go to Madang and be a gardener. I asked him why he returned to Arengin and he found it challenging to find the vocabulary, but I think the reason he came back was because he was homesick.

When we arrived, he took me to a house a little away from the village and told me this was to be my home and workplace. There was a large area of grass in front, which would be fine to use for teaching. There would be no desks or chairs, but that didn't matter.

A young woman arrived, and Albert introduced her as his sister Amali. It turned out that Father George was paying Albert to work for me whenever I needed him, and Amali for cooking and cleaning. When I suggested I could cook and clean myself, they both looked horrified and Amali burst out crying, obviously thinking that I meant she was not good enough for me. Her reaction made me realise how young she was, probably fourteen or fifteen and fast approaching marriage age. She was very pretty, and I was sure there would be plenty of young men hoping to catch hers and, more importantly, her mother's and father's eye. At least working for me, she could attend lessons and perhaps I could delay the inevitable.

I quickly reconsidered and told them I would be delighted for them to work for me.

The day was full of surprises. It turned out that not only were they working for me, but we were all going to be living in the same one room house. I had been in New Guinea long enough not to worry too much. We would find a way of organising things, so we all had our privacy.

Later that evening, two village elders, Bussi and Kutan, arrived to greet me formerly. I had met them both before and invited them to join me on the veranda for a chat and a smoke. Kutan's first question was quite surprising, however.

"Yu laik marit long meri Arengin?" (Would you like to marry a girl from Arengin?)

My first reaction was to ask which girl they had in mind, which showed that I hadn't quite lost my capacity for thinking foolish things. Fortunately, I allowed my brain time to work before opening my mouth. I politely declined and explained that marrying a local girl would be a delight and an honour. However, I would be returning to England at some point in the next year and it would not be fair to take my wife so far from her home and family or, the alternative, to abandon her. They understood and were happy with my answer.

I explained my plans to them. On weekdays, in the morning, I would run a school for young children who had never been before and could not speak tok pisin. I would teach them this and a little English, Maths and Art as well. They would then be ready to go to school in Giri the following year.

Early afternoon I would teach older children who were at school in Giri but, for some reason, had not attended every week. I assumed this would be mainly girls who were married or lived at home and were expected to work around the house and gardens, and whose parents would not want them to go to school every week.

In the evenings, I would be happy to teach tok pisin or English to older children who had never attended school, and also adults, on the condition that these sessions must be open for both men and women to attend.

I asked them to spread the word, and everyone who wished to attend one of the classes was to come anytime the next day so I could register them.

When the men had gone, Amali prepared her first meal for us. She was very nervous as we sat around the fire to eat. Albert had gone hunting during the day and had caught a small animal. I had no idea what it was, nor did I ask. We had some meat, green banana and yam, all baked on the fire. It was actually really good and when I told her that, she beamed and started laughing. It was infectious and soon Albert and I were laughing as well. I helped with the clearing up, which clearly was not something they felt was appropriate, but I explained that we were a team and, like it or not, I was going to muck in and help. Even this early in our relationship, I felt very comfortable with them and was sure we would become good friends.

The following day could have been a disaster. My worst fear was that no one would show any interest. In fact I ended up with nine boys and seven girls for the young children sessions. For the older children five girls and two boys and for the adults fifteen men and eleven women signed up. I knew that not all would actually attend and some would probably drop out but even so, I was really pleased with the response.

The next morning, I sent Albert and two others to Giri with the list of equipment I required. This included exercise books, pencils, colouring crayons, plain paper, a blackboard, an easel, chalk, dice, playing cards, any games that could be spared and as many sweets and chocolate bars that Father George was willing to donate from the mission shop. I knew the father would have to make the blackboard and easel, which would probably make him cross. I decided when I saw him next, I'd get in first and before he could say anything, tell him how everyone had admired the blackboard and easel and innocently ask him where he got them from.

In Giri, one of the rooms between the classrooms was used as a store for stuff that was never used, and I had noticed, a while back, some old cricket equipment there. Goodness knows where that came from. I asked for that to be sent as well.

A few evenings later, Amali hardly said a word while she was cooking and kept her back to me. I wondered if I had upset her. I asked Albert if anything was wrong as she was normally a real chatterbox. He told me that Amali was very upset. Arengin had suffered from much more rainfall than normal and many of the crops had failed. The bad weather also meant they had not been able to fetch salt from the coast and now there was none left. She felt she was letting me down and could not cook the things she wanted to. I told her not to worry; I could eat anything.

"No rat tasol." I added hastily. (No rat though)

I was reliant on the elders for organising gifts of food from the villagers, and the only thing that was plentiful was yam.

For the next seven weeks, ninety per cent of my diet was unsalted yam, morning, noon and night, wrapped in leaves, and cooked on the fire. I loved yam up to that point but by the end, I found it difficult to stomach and sadly still do.

A week after I arrived, classes started, rain allowing. Many more came than had registered, especially the little ones. They were gorgeous, happy, enthusiastic and always ready to laugh. They wore grass skirts, a type of sari or hand me down shorts and some had old, ripped shirts but most were bare topped. Their skin was chocolate brown and most had short black curly hair. Nearly all the children had pot bellies from their diet and spindly legs.

Amali and Albert were my classroom assistants, and once I had stopped Albert from slapping the pupils when he considered they were being naughty and Amali from cuddling them when she thought they were being nice, they were both brilliant.

We started with numbers. Each pupil was allocated a number; onepela, tupela, tripela, foapela, faivpela, sikispela, sevenpela, etpela, nainpela, tenpela.

Once you get beyond those numbers it's simple; sixteen is wanpela ten sikis, twenty three is tupella ten tri, and so on.

Every day the pupils had to add three to their number from the previous day and call it out in registration.

In the induction in Birmingham, we had had several sessions on Pidgin English. Our teacher never spoke to us in any other language. Nowadays it's called immersion learning. It was brilliant and I used this method in most of my teaching in Arengin. Only rarely asking Amali or Albert to translate an instruction into the local language.

The days were full of fun, with many physical and mental games being played. The younger one's favourite was an adaptation of grandmother's footsteps which nearly always ended up with everyone in a heap on the floor giggling like idiots. Sometimes the adults insisted that I play it with them as well.

Teaching the adults was strange, there were many betel nut and tobacco breaks but even so within a few weeks they were picking up the rudiments of tok pisin. The women were better scholars than the men by far.

Quite a lot of people came and watched the lessons and the number of participants definitely increased.

During the first teaching day, I had taught all the classes to play an adaptation of I Spy. That evening, after eating, Amali and Albert asked if we could play. This was the start of a regular event: playing some sort of game after eating. Another favourite was making up songs and tunes. Amali had a beautiful voice, whereas Albert thought he could sing well but was actually terrible. Amali and I did our best not to laugh but sometimes failed. On those occasions, Albert got in a bit of a huff. It never lasted long though.

Sometime in mid December, I stopped all lessons for Christmas. On the last day all the children were given a few sweets or a piece of chocolate and the adults got a couple of Australian cigarettes or some newspaper. If this sounds like a bribe, you'd be right; I wanted them back after Christmas.

The next day, I introduced the big Christmas event. The Cricket Match. I think if I had announced a 'who can get bitten most by mosquitoes' competition, there would have been far more enthusiasm. However, I expected that, after all, they had never even heard of cricket.

The day came and thirty or so men and a few women turned up to play. The rest of the village came to watch.

I explained the game as simply as I could, but it made me realise that tok pisin was not designed with the nuances of cricket in mind. Albert and Amali translated as best they could into the Arengin language.

I split them into two teams and fortunately, two strong young men agreed to open the batting. I opened the bowling. There were no pads or gloves so I decided we would use a rubber ball; It was hard but nothing like a proper cricket ball.

I marked out my run up, about ten yards, and hurtled in. Just as I was about to release the ball, there was a scream from the batsman, and he and most of the fielders at that end of the pitch ran into the bush as if a wild boar was on their tails.

It was chaos; the fielders that were left and all the spectators were either shouting at the fleeing villagers or rolling around screaming with laughter. It took half an hour to get everyone back. I swapped the rubber ball for an old tennis ball and demonstrated how soft it was by getting Albert to throw it at my chest. He missed and I spent the next five minutes rolling around on the ground in agony. My audience tried hard not to giggle. Actually, not that hard as I recall.

I bravely asked him to try again from a bit closer in. This time, his aim was good but actually, it hurt quite a lot, and I felt he didn't have to put quite that much effort into it, but I gritted my teeth, smiled and pretended everything was fine.

I tried to get them to start again, but no one was willing to bat until Amali became the hero of the day. She strode to the wicket and promptly belted my first ball, which was a rather fine in swinging yorker, straight into the bush for six. It took ten minutes to find it. I can only put it down to beginner's luck.

The game lasted a few hours. All the players had a go at batting and bowling, and I think everybody had a good, if somewhat bewildering, time. There was lots of laughter and plenty of advice from the spectators. No one, including me, had the faintest idea who had won.

The following day, I went to collect the bats and stumps but they had gone. I found their remains at Kutan's house. He had assumed they were finished with and used them as firewood. All that remained was ashes. Irony somewhere?

Years later, I wrote to the president of the MCC, (deadly) Derek Underwood, and told him that I had introduced cricket to the Middle Ramu in Papua New Guinea. I hoped he would invite me to join. Sadly, I never received a reply.

A few days before Christmas day, Father George arrived riding Giri. He took an outdoor service and gave Holy Communion. He checked to see if I was coming to Giri for Christmas Day and once I told him I wasn't, he asked me if I would do something on the day, even if it was just a prayer. I said I would. We shook hands, and he was gone.

Despite the dire diet, those months in Arengin were one of the happiest and most fulfilling periods of my life.

Sadly, it was about to come to a wretched end.

Me with some of my afternoon Arengin pupils
(I think I must have only had the one shirt)

Chapter 17   Sickness and Death

I had lived in Arengin for a few weeks when a young man came to see me. He said his name was Jonas and he had a small hut some way outside the village. He was a medical orderly and had been in Arengin for just over a year. He dispensed medicines and plasters and gave advice on health matters. He could speak a little bit of English but was more comfortable with tok pisin. He originally came from a village a few miles from Madang.

Until then, I had no idea there was a person doing medicine in the village. Apparently, he had been appointed by the hospital in Madang. Following nearly six months of training, he was posted to Arengin. Although he was based there, he regularly did clinics in other villages to the south and was away most of the time. He said that I would be welcome, if I ever wanted, to join him when he did his rounds.

I asked him how he got fresh supplies. He said it was not a regular thing, but every few months, a visiting doctor or patrol officer would come through one of his villages, usually on horseback, and drop off basic materials.

I was becoming increasingly fond of Amali and Albert. They were great fun, always laughing about something or other and chatting away in the local language. Then, they would notice I was listening and apologise for not including me. I told them I didn't mind and that I could understand some of what they were saying. It wasn't actually true, but I was just happy being in their company.

In the evening, we would sit by the fire in front of the house telling stories, playing games or discussing how the lessons had gone and, when it was fully dark, retired to bed. We each slept on a blanket on the floor, I was in one corner and they were near each other in the opposite corner. As Amali was getting ready for bed, she would often hum a tune or quietly sing a song. I loved that and often fell asleep to the sound of her voice. I felt rather sad that by the time she was sixteen, this outgoing, intelligent girl would be married and her whole life would be centred around her husband, having children and the drudgery of village life. She probably saw it quite differently, however.

As Christmas approached, one or two people began to get sick. They had sore throats and coughs. It did not seem to be serious, and on Christmas Day, I supervised a low key, outdoor service. We said some prayers, and the children who went to school in Giri and those I had taught in Arengin sang carols they had learnt. I read part of the Christmas story from my Nupela Testamen; all the volunteers had been given a copy when we first arrived in Alexishafen. It was the complete new testament translated into tok pisin.

After the service, there was a football match and games for the children. It was a nice, gentle day.

That evening, I felt quite low. Amali and Albert were spending the evening with their family. I hoped my mum and dad were OK and having a nice time. I wished I could speak to them, wish them a happy Christmas and tell them I love them.

My heart had been heavy for the last few days and I couldn't work out why. It felt as if something bad was happening or about to happen, but there was nothing really untoward in the village. I tried to ignore the feeling but slept fitfully.

A few days later, Jonas came to see me. He told me that he had gone to one of his villages, Puk, to do his clinic, and when he arrived, a nun had been waiting for him. She was a nurse and had said that a disease was making people ill all over Papua New Guinea, and some were dying. She had given him some medicine and showed him how to use it. He was going to treat three people now and wanted me to come with him and learn how to do it.

He told me that the disease was a strain of the Asian flu, and the medicine was a form of penicillin.

Much later, I was to discover the strain was the Hong Kong variant and the type of penicillin was benzathine G.

The injection was painful as a large amount had to be injected into the rump of the bottom, forming a sizeable lump. It then gradually was absorbed into the body. Not only did it hurt but there was no guarantee it would work.

Jonas insisted I did one, an old man with little flesh to inject into. It was horrible for both of us; he was screaming at one point.

Jonas was soon busy in all his villages administering the penicillin and trying to persuade people to mix with other families as little as possible.

Over the following weeks, more and more people became sick and I closed the school. As well as the other symptoms, they became very weak and achy, and some developed dangerously high fevers. Some of the children had nosebleeds, which were hard to control.

160

I woke one morning and was told that an older woman and a young boy had died during the night; neither had had the injection.

Over the next few days, more people died, and the villagers began to get angry. They felt they were being given bad medicine and not getting good treatment. Albert told me that people were blaming Jonas; some suspected he was deliberately killing people with magic and others just thought he was incompetent.

I went to warn Jonas, but there was no sign of him; he had left with all his things apart from the medical equipment. I guessed that he feared for his life. I wondered whether, when he insisted that I learn how to administer the treatment, he realised, even then, that this could happen and he would need to escape one day.

The village elders asked me to help as I knew how to administer the penicillin. Of course, I agreed to do what I could.

There was an expectation from some that when I entered a home and administered medicine, everything would be fine; I was the white man from England sent by Father George. My magic was very strong. But it didn't happen like that. People died under my care and some of those had been treated with the penicillin. Two were children. I had never seen a dead body before and spent those weeks in a haze of misery, stumbling from one horror to another. Even though, in my heart, I knew I could not have done more, I still felt very guilty. I tried not to let my emotions overwhelm me until I was alone at night and then the sobs came.

The last person to die in the village was Amali. Early in the epidemic, her parents had come to fetch her and Albert, feeling that because I was visiting sick people, they would be safer at home. One night they came to fetch me and I could see that she was very ill. I immediately gave her an injection and left her to sleep with instructions they should try to keep her cool with wet rags. I prayed for her that night.

The next morning, I woke early and in the semi-darkness, I could see Albert in the doorway, and I knew immediately why he was there. I walked across the room, took him into my arms and held him as tightly as I could. In the silence of the dawn, we held each other and wept. He returned to his family and I sat in the hut on the blanket that Amali had slept on and cried and prayed.

In my whole life, I have never felt so desolate and alone as I was then.

The people of Arengin did not really know how to cope with what had happened. Nearly everyone in the village had lost a close relative or friend. They rarely showed extreme outward emotion and their way of dealing with a tragedy was to find the person responsible and to be proactive. This was too big, and they were lost.

Gradually, as time passed, fewer people became ill, and those who did seem to have less serious symptoms. There were no further deaths. I thought about reopening the school but my heart wasn't in it and nobody tried very hard to persuade me.

Albert decided to go to Madang to make his fortune and I wrote him a letter that he could give to prospective employers saying he was a good worker and a fine young man.

He left on a Monday morning in March and I never heard from him again.

Following the epidemic, I was treated very differently. Any aura I had had because of my background, race or culture was gone. I was a person like any other, no better, no worse and no hidden magic. I do not think they blamed me for the deaths. They saw the emotion in me and knew how upset I was; I couldn't hide it. I just hoped they knew that I had done my best.

I do not see myself as a practical person but I tried to help where I could. I went to families who had lost someone and helped in the garden or collected water and firewood. Or just talked to them where possible. In return, they gave me some food or sometimes invited me to eat with them.

Looking back now, I realised that I was truly part of their community for the first time since coming to New Guinea.

Years later, I told a nursing friend about what had happened. She said I was very brave to do what I did, knowing I might catch the disease and die. Her words really shook me. I wasn't brave at all; the truth is, until she said that, it had never once occurred to me that I might catch it. I wonder what would have happened, had I realised back then.

At the end of 1969 and into 1970, it is estimated that, worldwide, up to three and a half million people died from the Hong Kong variant of Asian flu. It is, therefore, likely that tens of thousands died in Papua New Guinea. It was particularly bad in remote areas who received no help from outside.

Chapter 18 Farewell

In March 1970, I became ill. The Asian flu had abated so, from what I was told later, it was almost certain that I had malaria. I had not taken any malaria tablets since the day I arrived in Kuala Lumpur.

I had a fever, was confused and delusional, couldn't walk properly and was not eating or drinking. Over several days, I got progressively worse; I lost my sense of reality and was almost never fully conscious.

Seven days after first becoming ill, I woke up. I was in bed in my old room in Giri, and sitting next to me was Bonnie. He was so happy to see I was awake. He fussed about and finally went off to tell Father George.

He came back after a few minutes to say that the father was making some soup, and in the meantime, I was to drink plenty of water.

Father George arrived looking relieved. He could see that I was recovering well and looked so much better. He told me that, two days earlier, someone had banged on his door in the middle of the night. When he came out, there was just me wrapped in an old blanket, unconscious on the floor of his veranda. All my possessions, such as they were, were next to me.

The following day, my fever was out of control, and he feared I might die. There was nothing he could do. The nearest medical centre was Bogia and he didn't think I would survive the journey. However, the next night, the fever had broken and I was breathing properly and appeared to be sleeping peacefully.

He told me that Bonnie had stayed by my side throughout; he had had to shout at him to get him to go and get a few hours' sleep.

He had no idea how I had been brought to Giri and said that carrying me so far in that terrain was extraordinary, but to do it at night was beyond belief. Whoever did it almost certainly saved my life. Father George thought they must have been desperately concerned for me and probably worried about the consequences of me dying in Arengin, thinking they would be blamed. I thought it more likely they were being kind; I hope so anyway. I never did find out who my guardian angels were.

I decided enough was enough; it was time to go home. Father George wrote to the mission headquarters and arrangements were made. The money VSO had given for the journey was enough to get me to New Zealand where I could stay with my brother, Gordon and his family.

In the week before I left, I made sure that I visited all the people who had become so much part of my life. Needless to say, tears were shed, mainly by me. I was given many gifts, including two kundu drums, one from my papa in Giri Number 2, beautifully carved, and the other from Bonnie and Hans. They had made it themselves and it was quite rough but it was the best present I'd ever been given. I hugged them until they were thoroughly embarrassed. I shared the few dollars I had left with them and Joseph and Abi in Giri. Joseph gave me a bird of paradise feather. He also gave me his watch which had stopped working and asked if I would get it repaired.

I received quite a few wooden carvings as well; some very rough and some beautifully made. They were all precious. Most were of animals, mainly crocodiles and snakes, but also small ceremonial masks. I handed out chocolate and newspaper.

Sadly, I never got to say goodbye to the people of Arengin, and I have always regretted that.

On my last night, I had dinner with Jim and Father George and a final game of chess. I thought he might let me win but he was as ruthless as ever. He told me about the arrangements for my journey. In the morning, there would be a leaving ceremony where villagers would sing and dance for me and prepare a special meal. He would then drive me to Mikarew, and Brother Vasavious would take me on to Bogia. From there, I had requested that I be allowed to fly to Mount Hagen for a few days and then on to Sydney via Port Moresby. I was to stay overnight in the YMCA and fly to Auckland the following morning.

Later, I joined Jim and the teachers and spent a happy few hours chatting and listening to them sing and play their guitars. I had my last ever betel nut.

It was wonderful to see the great friendship that had formed between all of them, and it was clear how much they liked and respected Jim.

It had rained a lot over the last week and that night was no exception. In the morning, Father George took the Unimog out to check the road and an hour later came back looking very unhappy.

"There is no chance of any vehicles getting through to Mikarew," he said.

"I could ride," I suggested.

"No, definitely not. The rivers are like torrents; a horse could never cross safely. You will have to walk."

I realised I would have to leave much earlier and would definitely miss the feast, which was probably no bad thing. The last thing I needed was a tummy bug on the plane.

I walked to the various groups congregating around the mission to see if they could bring forward the dance and music. Giri people do not like to be hurried however, and nothing seemed to be happening, so I decided just to go.

I was very concerned about my suitcase. It was cumbersome and very heavy with all the gifts I had received. I also had two kundus which didn't fit in the case, and I really didn't want to leave anything behind. I struggled to carry it all a hundred yards, so how on earth would I get it to Mikarew?

Father George was nowhere to be seen, but a man, two women and a girl approached me. The man told me that the father had asked him to come with me and carry the suitcase. He introduced me to his two wives, Ruth and Ilundu and his daughter Joana.

Bonnie wanted to come with us, but I said no. Bonnie was elderly, overweight and definitely not fit. I could see us having to carry him as well.

I was upset and disappointed that Father George had not seen me off, but as we passed the church, he came out and beckoned me over. He told me that he had already agreed on a payment with the people for carrying the case and would settle the debt when they returned. Then he asked me to follow him into the church.

What happened next was utterly out of character and left me in a very emotional state.

Father George said he wanted to pray with me. We both knelt at the altar. In English, he said a prayer wishing me a safe journey and a happy and successful life. He then indicated that I should join him in saying the Lord's prayer in tok pisin.

We left the church. He shook my hand, gave me a brief hug and walked away. I cannot explain why but tears were pouring down my cheeks. Somehow it was symbolic and it marked the end of my time in Giri and

in Papua New Guinea. In all probability, I would never
return.

<u>The Lord's Prayer</u>
*Papa belong mipela, yu i stap long heven, nem belong
yu i mas i stap holi.*
*Kingdom belong yu i mas i kam. Laik belong yu ol
bihainim long heven, olsem tasol mipela i mas
bihainim long graun tu.*
Nau yu givim mipela kaikai inap long dispela de.
*Na yu lusim ol sin belong mipela, olsem mipelatu i
lusim pinis sin belong ol man i bin rongim mipela.*
*Na yu no bingim mipela long samting belong traim
mipela, tasol tekewe mipela long samting nogut.*
*Kingdom na strong na glori, em i belong yu tasol
oltaim oltaim tru.*   *Amen*

<u>The Lord's Prayer</u>
Our Father, who art in heaven,
hallowed be thy name;
thy kingdom come;
thy will be done;
on earth as it is in heaven.
Give us this day our daily bread.
And forgive us our trespasses,
as we forgive those who trespass against us.
And lead us not into temptation;
but deliver us from evil.
For thine is the kingdom,
the power and the glory,
for ever and ever.
Amen.

A Kundu Drum, similar, but much longer than the ones I was given.

Chapter 19   Father George

Until the day I left Giri, Father George had not given the impression of being a warm or friendly man, either to the people he served as priest or me. He seemed happy with his own company and I rarely saw him visit Giri or other villages in his charge, apart from when he took mass. Most of his interaction with the indigenous people was in church, at the store or when they worked for him.

Every day he attended the flag ceremony before school, but he never visited classrooms unless he was giving a talk, and I never knew him to attend a Sing Sing or for that matter participate in any communal activities in the villages.

He was responsible for my welfare, so I believe, yet he did nothing to help me in those first few terrible months. In fact, the opposite was true; he made me feel useless and unwanted. He gave me tasks I was incapable of doing and with minimal guidance. I didn't expect anything from him at the time, but I realised later that he could have helped me enormously and saved me a great deal of pain.

And yet, even though I had shown myself to be inept or worse, when the opportunity came for him to be able to get shot of me, he fought for me instead.

When I decided to stay, nothing changed. He continued to give me tasks that I thought were beyond my capabilities, yet I managed.

I ended up having a wonderful time, being a useful member of the community, achieving much and growing up in many ways, or so I believe. Perhaps the way he behaved was right, but on the other hand, I believe it could have gone horribly wrong. I think it would have scarred me for life if I'd gone home or left for another mission in those early months.

However, in the back of my mind, there is a thought that if he had been a warmer person and I had genuinely bonded with him, perhaps I would have spent more time on the mission and not had the incredible experiences I had in Giri and the other villages; perhaps I would never have ended up spending months in Arengin. Who knows?

After mass, he always opened the store and his rule was that only those who had attended the service could buy things. He was sometimes rude to the customers and there were no pleasantries. One Sunday, after the sale of a tin of fish, I saw him take the money and then throw the tin out of the door onto the ground. It may have been that the man had done or said something that he found rude, although I was not aware of anything. Even so, I thought then and I think now, it was disrespectful and wrong; it set the wrong kind of example. There were other incidents that were similar to this. I don't think it was a race issue. After all he often treated me in the same way.

The station had a Honda 50 motorbike, with especially low gears for the local terrain. In dry weather, I was sometimes sent to Mikarew to collect or take post or pick up small supplies that had been brought that far from Bogia. The first three times I went out on it, I ran out of petrol on the way back and had to walk the rest of the way to the station. I always felt somehow that I had done something very wrong; it was humiliating. Father George would take a container of petrol and walk out and collect it and he always insisted on doing it himself. On the third occasion, I had got to within a few hundred yards of the mission. I followed him and was surprised to see that, instead of putting petrol in, he leaned over and pulled a small lever next to the petrol tank. When I asked him about it, he said it allowed petrol to go into the tank from a backup reservoir. To this day I cannot think of a reason why he would feel the need to keep this from me.

The worst thing I saw him do was truly shocking.

It appeared that Bonnie's dog, Manham, had some kind of skin condition that may or may not have been contagious to humans. It was Bonnie's only actual possession, and he loved it; it meant so much to him.

One day, I was teaching in my classroom when I heard a commotion and Bonnie ran into the room. He was crying and completely distraught.

"masta, pater i got raifol. Em i laik kilim manam, kilim i dai. Yu passim pater." (The father has a rifle, he wants to kill Manham, kill him dead. You stop him)

At that point, we heard a gunshot. I ran out of the room and saw Manham come tearing out of one classroom and into another. The dog was obviously terrified and panicking. Father George ran after him and fired into the room three times. Manham let out an awful yelping howl and then went quiet. Children from both rooms were hysterical; some ran out screaming. These kids had all seen animals killed, but the intense violence of this event and the lack of any kind of compassion were extraordinary.

Bonnie ran into the room and came out carrying his dead friend. Father George walked nonchalantly away without speaking.

Up to then, I had never talked to Father George in a critical way or questioned his decisions, but that evening, I told him how bad that had been for Manham, Bonnie and the children, some of whom had been seriously traumatised. During the past six months, the classroom floors had been improved and made more permanent using concrete. I pointed out that the bullets could have ricocheted off the concrete and injured or even killed one of the pupils. He listened without comment and then turned the conversation to something else. I had no idea whether he agreed or felt any remorse, but he never mentioned it again, and that was the end of the incident.

Most of the time, Father George was a cold man towards humans but seemed to love inanimate objects, especially when he could fix or tinker with them. The unimog was his pride and joy and despite his comments on the way to Giri the first time, I was never allowed to drive it. Something I was very happy with.

Then, out of the blue, he showed such compassion and warmth in the church as I was leaving Giri for the last time, something I had not thought him capable of.

I do not want to make him out as a bad man or a bad priest, and he wasn't. If anyone was sick, they could go to him day or night, and he would always do his best to treat them. He was always trying to improve the school and mission and did a lot of physical work to that end. Watching him take mass you could see and hear the conviction of his beliefs; he was inspiring.

Perhaps one of the best and kindest things he did was keeping Bonnie as his cook and housekeeper. Bonnie was a terrible cook, and his sense of hygiene was truly frightening. Father knew that sacking Bonnie would leave him with nothing and nowhere to go.

He was a good man and a good priest in many ways but I believe he had faults and did some bad things.

Sheila came to Giri a year after I had left, and for some time, another young woman, Gwendolyn, was with her. In her excellent book 'Memoirs of a Volunteer,' Sheila wrote,

'Father George had really been a friend to us. He was a great personality, lively and young in temperament. He made us completely at ease. He was warm, respectful and childish too. I think he quite liked having "his ladies" in Giri, often getting us to talk about boys!

The night before he left, we had a bit of a party and drank half a bottle of Benedictine, which we all liked. As usual we found ourselves talking about religion, the most exciting of topics. He seems to us to be a very down to earth and open person; unlike any other priest we had ever met.

When he'd gone, we felt very empty and found it difficult to keep our classes going.'

When I read this, I had to assure myself that this was the same Father George that I had known.

The volunteer who followed me, Jim, had a similar experience to mine; he also found the father cold, distant and unhelpful on a personal level.

174

Both Sheila and Gwendolyn talk of him smiling, laughing and having fun with him. I never saw that in my whole twenty month spell.

So why was he so different the following year? There are a number of possibilities.

The volunteers were a few years older and, therefore, a bit more mature and able to debate and discuss.
Some of the time there were two of them.
They were both women.
Sheila was a Catholic.
Both were graduates.
One had already been teaching in England.

Things had also changed at Giri mission; there were proper washing facilities, a medical centre and more modern classrooms. A shortwave radiotelephone had made it possible to communicate with the outside world.

Sheila and Gwendolyn also regularly went to Bogia, where they met other young people and participated in dances and other activities.

Father George left Giri in 1975 and worked at various missions. He was the priest at Mikarew from 1987 to 1992 and built a new church there.

When I returned to England, I received two letters from him. I am ashamed to say that I replied to the first but not the second and was not in contact with him again. It was not because I didn't want to reply, I just never got around to it; I was so tied up with my own life. I dearly wish I had.

Obituary

Jerzy Miozga, known also as George, was born in the village of Poczolkowo in the parish of Zebowice, in Opole County in Poland on 13th April 1933. He was admitted to Minor Seminary of the Society of the Divine Word in Nysa in August 1949. This was shut down by the communist authorities in 1952. That year he moved to Major Seminary in Pieniezno, in the north of Poland and begun his novitiate there.

He professed his religious vows in September 1954 and was ordained a priest on 29 January 1961 in Pieniezno. From 1961 till 1966 he worked in various parishes in Poland. On 17 September 1966 he left Poland for his mission in New Guinea. On the way he took an English course in Sydney, Australia which lasted a few months.

In May 1967 he landed in New Guinea and was sent to Mugil for introduction to mission work under the guidance of Fr. Hempelmann. Soon he was appointed by Archbishop Noser to the parish of Giri. He worked there from 1968 till 1975. He worked also in Megiar and Alexishafen. From 1987 till 1992 he worked at Mikarew and built a church there.

For a long time he had problems with his heart. He had a bypass operation in early years of 2000. In 2005 he arrived in Alexishafen and became District Superior.

On the 21st April 2007 he was on an annual retreat and became ill. An ambulance was called but before they reached the hospital in Madang he died of heart failure.

On 24th April the Archbishop William Kurtz presided over his funeral and he was buried at the Divine Word Missionaries cemetery at Alexishafen.

Father George   Father George and
the Honda 50

Bonnie. This picture was taken a
Year after I left. I wonder if Father
George had given him a new dog

177

Chapter 20   Pooh

When the man Rom had said he would carry my case, he really meant that his two wives, Ruth and Ilundu would carry it.

They were incredible; one of them put the case in a huge net which was then lifted onto her back with the handles of the net around her forehead. The two women swapped every five hundred yards or so. I offered to take a turn but all four of them looked at me as if I was crazy and said no. Ruth laughed out loud at such an idea. She was given a stern look by Ilundu, who was obviously the boss wife. I guess they did not think me physically capable, and they were almost certainly right.

It was the most difficult of journeys. It rained constantly and we regularly had to leave the road because of flooding. The hilly parts were slippery and crossing the rivers was seriously hazardous, especially the log bridges where the slightest mistake could cause a leg to slip between the logs with every chance of a broken ankle or worse. All told I think we walked eight miles and it took nearly six hours. Just as we reached Mikarew, the rain stopped, the clouds disappeared and the sun blazed down.

Rom and his family decided to stay in Mikarew and travel back the next day. They were hoping everything would be dryer by morning. Brother Vasavious was anxious to get going; He wanted to be back before it was too dark. I thanked my travelling companions profusely, jumped into the jeep and we were off.

Most of the low points in my life before leaving for New Guinea were associated with the schools I attended, which, apart from a few great teachers, I found gave me nothing but a feeling of failure. The high points of my life happened when I was attending cubs, scouts and venture scouts. I loved the discipline, the order, the excitement, the physicality and the friendships.

I belong to the 7th Woking group when I was in the scouts and our leader was Mr Rawlings. He had been an officer in the Gurkha Regiment.

He taught us how to work together but also be self-sufficient. I remember vividly the wonderful wide games, incident night hikes and the camps. We regularly went to a place called Sheets Heath, near Brookwood, for camping. We would meet at the scout hut early in the morning. The trek cart; a heavy two wheeled vehicle with a long handle, was loaded with the tents, equipment and our own rucksacks and we then pulled it over four miles to the campsite.

We were responsible for everything. Each patrol of six erected their tent, cooked, made gadgets, dug toilet pits and much more. It was all about discipline and working together as a team.

Each morning at 7 am, we would be woken by Mr Rawlings putting his head in the tent and shouting,

"Wakey wakey, anyone want to buy a trek cart?"

We regularly discussed ways of assassinating him as we got dressed.

After breakfast, we were inspected and so was our tent and kit. There was great rivalry between the patrols and points were awarded for many things including the inspection.

In 1965, six of us became venture scouts led by the aforementioned Rod (Rabbit) Taylor. He was a formidable leader. He cajoled us into doing things that we didn't really think we were capable of. I have no recollection of him ever being violent but you felt it was never far away. We loved and hated him in equal measures, well truth be told, more love than hate. We undoubtedly respected him.

The reason is now long lost in history, but we were all given names from Winnie the Pooh.

My special friend was Richard, who was known as Pooh. I think and hope it was because he liked honey. Raldon was clever and sensible, so he had to be Wol. On a hike across Dartmoor, I gained a blister on one foot and hopped. The following day I got one on the other foot and bounced and thus I became Tigger.

It was quite extraordinary but Pooh and I both found out we would be going to New Guinea, a country we knew nothing about, within a week of each other and for entirely different reasons. Pooh was going to work for his uncle who owned a coffee plantation in Mount Hagen. He would be setting out a few weeks ahead of me.

Just before leaving, we camped at Durdle Door campsite in Dorset and had a great week exploring the coastline in canoes.

I had no money as usual and expected to live on bread and the odd beer. Pooh would have none of it, and every evening we drove to the Castle Inn in West Lulworth to listen to Fire by Arthur Brown on the jukebox and eat pie and chips and down a few beers. Pooh was the most generous person I have ever met.

After years in New Guinea, he moved to Australia, where he still lives. We have met up only twice in the last fifty years, but I still think of him as a very special friend.

I stayed with him in Mount Hagen for just a few days. While writing this book, I contacted him and asked him what we did and saw. He couldn't actually remember and neither can I. I suspect we spent most of the time chatting, reminiscing and making up songs that basically made fun of Rabbit, who now lives in South Africa.

The one that we were most proud of was sung to the tune of Jingle Bells.

Bouncing through the grass, Tigger flashes past
Faraway Wol flew, for to see young Pooh
Pooh was having tea, honey running free
Rabbit's running through a bog
Fleeing from a dog

Oh, Tigger's here, Pooh is here
Let's all shout hurray
Wol is flitting all around
And everybody's gay
Oh, Pooh is here, Tigger's here
Let's all kneel and pray
Everybody's happy
Cos Rabbit's passed away

Childish, silly, embarrassing. Yes, all those things. But for two young men who were the greatest of friends, sitting on a veranda, deep in the bush, eight thousand miles from home, knowing they would quite possibly never meet again, well, it just seemed the right thing to do.

One incident I do remember, is that one morning when driving into town to get provisions, Pooh stopped the jeep as there was steam coming from under the bonnet. He got a can of water and topped up the radiator.

I noticed a local man with an interesting headdress a little way down the road. I wandered over and asked him if I could take his picture. He nodded and faced the camera. After I had taken it, he approached me and, rather aggressively, demanded a dollar. Nothing changes, I still had no money. I showed him my empty pockets, but he just kept repeating onepela dola. I told the man to stay put, went over to Pooh and asked him if I could borrow a dollar. He said it was ridiculous to pay him that much, but I knew I should have made it clear how much I would give him, if anything, before taking the photograph. Pooh gave me the money.

I'll pay him back one day.

Sheets Heath – 7th
Woking Scout Group
Morning Inspection
before going swimming

* The dreaded trek cart

Pooh looking as
handsome as ever

Mount Hagen
Onepela Dola Photo

*Photograph by kind permission of Richard Llewellyn,
1st Blackwater Valley B-P Scout Group

Not for the faint hearted

This was told to me by an Australian patrol officer. He would not say where in New Guinea he and his colleagues had discovered it. He said that it was happening as late as 1964, and they had done their best to put a stop to it. However, it is possible it could still be happening (in 1969) in some remote villages.

When a woman has her first child, a ceremony takes place. The woman will take her baby to a nearby stream or river. People from her village will accompany her and one of them will bring a pig with its recently born piglets.

A village elder will help the woman ask for guidance from her ancestors and then she will take her baby to a rocky place on the edge of the water. She will then take her child by one leg, swing it around, and smash its head on the rocks.

The dead baby is then placed on a bed of reeds or a simple boat made of twigs and allowed to float away.

The woman must then choose one of the piglets and bring it up as if it were her own child, including breastfeeding it.

She will be judged not on her future children but on the health and strength of the piglet that she suckled.

Chapter 21   The Journey Home

<u>Australia</u>

I reached Sydney and walked the mile or so from the airport to the YMCA. My case was being transferred onto the Auckland plane for the morning, so I didn't have to worry about that.

There was a pub a few doors down and, in the evening, I dropped in really just for something to do. I sat on a stool at the bar and ordered a Coca-Cola. Two young men were sitting nearby and one approached and asked me if I was a girl. I wasn't too sure if I'd heard him right.

"Sorry, I don't really understand what you're asking," I said.

"Oi Bob, he's not just a girl. He's a pom girl. Why don't I give him a few bruises to take home with him."

He lifted his fist, but the barman had come round and placed himself between us.

"You're not starting any trouble in my bar Cameron Curtis, now go and sit down." He turned to me.

"Here's your money back. You're not safe here; find somewhere else to have a drink."

I walked out feeling very confused.

<u>New Zealand</u>

The next day I arrived in Auckland. As I went through customs, my case was opened and the contents examined. The officer told me that because the kundus had skins, they would not be allowed to enter New Zealand. Also, some of the wooden artefacts had signs of infestation, they would not be allowed in either. I was devastated. I pleaded, but the best the officer could do was to say that I could have them back

185

on leaving the country, which at least gave me some hope.

My brother and his family were there to meet me and took me to their home in the suburb of Birkdale. I stayed for nearly two weeks.

I loved meeting and being with my brother Gordon, his wife, Julia and their young children Richard, Peter and Catherine, but I do not think I was an easy guest to have. I had been nearly two years living in primitive conditions in a truly alien culture. Adapting was hard and I found Auckland daunting. My first experience of an automatic opening shop door almost caused me to jump back into the path of a double-decker bus.

The family wanted to take me out and show me things. The problem was that I was desperately tired and mixed up, and felt I needed to be on my own much of the time.

However, we did a camping holiday in Rotorua and other places where Māori culture was explained and honoured. I really enjoyed that.

Before leaving Mount Hagen, Pooh and I had hatched a plan as to how I might get back to the UK. On arrival in New Zealand, I put my name down to work my passage home on a boat. The idea was that if one of the crew jumped ship, they could call on you with very little notice to take their place. After two weeks, I was contacted and agreed to board the following afternoon. The whole family saw me off and Gordon told me I was always welcome to come back, and that he would contact the authorities and try to get them to send on the things that had been quarantined. Sadly, for whatever reason, it never happened and I lost all those items including the kundus.

I went up the steps onto the deck and waved. They waved back and walked away. I never saw my brother again, he died of a heart attack some years later. I have met Julia and my niece Cath on a number of occasions since, both in New Zealand and England. They are truly wonderful people and I love them dearly. I just wish I had been a better guest back then in 1970.

The Merchant Navy
The SS Piako was a part of the New Zealand Shipping Line fleet. It was a cargo boat that carried frozen meat, mainly lamb, around the world. It had a crew of around twenty. The person I replaced was the engineer's steward, and that would be the job I was to take on. I was shown to my cabin by two young lads, Alfie and George, who were actual cabin boys; I thought they only existed in books! They both looked about sixteen years old but said they were older. They told me I was to wait for the bosun to come and see me.

My cabin was small but not tiny. It comprised of a single bed, a desk and a chair. There was also a toilet and sink in the corner with a thin cardboard wall surrounding them. I was massively relieved to find that I was not sharing. Apparently, on passenger boats, the crew are often squeezed together in tiny cabins but cargo boat crew fare much better.

A while later, a man in uniform knocked on the door. He introduced himself as Neville, the bosun of the ship. He said he had to take care of something and I was to meet him on deck in ten minutes, on the port side. He looked at me to ensure I knew what that meant. I nodded.

I walked up to the deck and watched the preparations taking place for our departure. A tall thin man wandered up to me.

"Hi, I'm Bill. Your new!" I introduced myself and shook his hand. "Welcome aboard; you'll love it here; everyone is really friendly. I work in the galley, sort of chef's assistant. If you need any help, come and see me anytime." He wandered away. Brilliant, I had someone I could go to when stuck or needing advice.

Soon afterwards, Neville walked up.

"Right, Richard. I am the ship's bosun, basically in charge of discipline and ensuring the work gets done properly and safely and nobody shirks and, also, to keep those cabin boys out of mischief. When you talk to me, you call me Bosun. Anything you want to ask me first?" I shook my head.

"Good, I'm going to give you two pieces of advice. Firstly, I saw you chatting with Bill earlier. He is the nicest, friendliest guy imaginable. When he's sober. When he's had too many drinks, he's a monster and very dangerous. Last year he was in a ship out of Melbourne and after drinking all evening he met the baker who made a joke at his expense. Bill dragged him to the galley and held his hand in boiling fat until he passed out. So, if you see him and you think he's had a few, report to me or any officer and then lock yourself in your room. Do not talk to him."

"But why do you employ him?" I asked, feeling a little alarmed.

"Well, he's wanted by the police in just about every port we go to. So, he never goes ashore. When he gets to the final destination he simply gets on another boat, he never leaves the dock and that way he doesn't enter the country. He just leaves one ship and gets on another. Because of that, he doesn't spend much of his wages, so I think he bribes the recruitment officers.

That's the first thing. Secondly, keep a low profile, listen rather than talk and never, never ever get involved in an argument about politics, football, religion or Ireland. Got it?"

I nodded.

"Right, I'm going to show you around and tell you what's expected."

He gave me a tour. On the bridge, I met some of the officers, including the first mate. We then went to the mess where meals were taken, the galley, the engine room and the engineer's corridor. There were eight engineers who looked after the ship's engines and the massive freezers in the hold.

He explained my duties. My job each day was to clean their corridor, each of their rooms, toilets and washrooms, and other duties that would be given to me on the day.

My working day started at 7.30, just after breakfast, and didn't finish until after 7 in the evening when an inspection would take place, usually by the captain. If all was well, that meant spotless, I could go for dinner but if not, I worked on until an officer had the time and the inclination to re-inspect the work.

We had an hour for lunch and two half hour breaks, one in the morning and one in the afternoon.

Finally, he said, "Oh, by the way, whenever you meet an officer, there is no need to salute unless you want to but always stand to attention. Some of them don't care but some of them get a bit narky if you don't. Now Merchantman Masters, You're in the merchant navy now, be proud."

When he was certain that I had understood everything, he relaxed.

"I'm sure you'll be fine; in a few days we'll be docking in Brisbane."

"Brisbane?" I said, rather alarmed, "I thought we were going to London."

He laughed. "We are, but there are a few stops on the way. Don't worry lad, the food's good and the pay isn't bad."

That was the first time it even occurred to me that I was being paid.

The food was more than good; it was amazing; steak, lamb chops, steak and kidney pudding and plenty more were always on offer. Roast rat and sago were conspicuous by their absence. I told some of my shipmates about the food in New Guinea but I don't think they really believed me.

I didn't make any friends but got on quite well with everyone. The officers ate separately, and I didn't really get to know any of them.

Someone told me that Neville had fought in the Second World War and been captured. He'd spent a long time in a Japanese prisoner of war camp. One day I asked him about it and he simply said that he still had nightmares and it was not something he had ever talked about to anyone. He doubted that he ever would.

The work was physically demanding, and the hours were long but that was OK. I was a bit nervous with the first inspection but actually it was pretty cursory and the captain didn't really look very hard. He stood too close when talking to me for my liking and I could smell alcohol on his breath. I admit to taking an instant dislike to him. He was not popular with any of the crew as far as I could tell.

Alfie and George

I soon got used to the rhythm of life on board and quite enjoyed it. Alfie and George were regular companions. I think it was because I was closer to their age than most, but also, I was new and they could show off to me. I was shocked by the things they had experienced in various ports, even if only half of them were true. They prided themselves on being experts on the seediest places to visit wherever the ship docked. They desperately tried to persuade me to join them in Brisbane. They knew several clubs where the music was loud, the booze was cheap, and it was easy to pick up a girl for the night. And, if all else failed, there was a brothel just up the road, which was one of the cheapest they had ever encountered.

I did think about it, but not for long. A fun night with Alfie and George seemed to me to be a recipe for disaster, and I wasn't brave enough.

After Brisbane, we sailed to Sydney, back to Brisbane, then to Auckland and only then did we head for home. I never left the ship. What a coward!

Homeward Bound

We set off from Auckland for the final time and the next stop was London. Three weeks in, I received some worrying news. Alfie told me that there was an old merchant navy tradition that when you crossed the equator for the first time, you were stripped of all your clothes and your hair was completely shaved off. You were then tied in a chair and the chair was lowered into the sea on the end of a rope. You were dunked several times and then pulled back up again. Both he and George had gone through this. Crossing the equator was only a few days away.

I explained that I had already crossed the equator on the way to New Guinea, so surely, I would not have to go through this horrid ritual. Alfie was not too sure about that but he thought you had to cross it in a boat for it to count.

I decided to avoid this if I could and went to the Baker, who doubled as the Barber and got him to give me a really short crew cut; no harm in making myself less conspicuous.

On the day the ship was due to cross the equator, I had no meals. When I wasn't working, I stayed in my cabin with the door barricaded. Nothing happened. The following morning, I asked the bosun if Alfie had been pulling my leg.

"Jim O'Reilly was the chap you replaced who jumped ship in Auckland," told me, "he was the Union Rep and had he been on the boat, you wouldn't have got on at all. The unions are trying to stop people doing what you did; amateurs working their way home. He also loved and upheld the traditions, and you would have certainly gone naked, hairless and overboard. I think you are a lucky boy Merchantman Masters."

Thirty five days in, we passed through the Panama Canal. Those not on duty stood on the deck and waved at the people on the shore. They looked pretty ragged and some of the crew threw coins and food, another tradition.

At one point, we watched a fight between two men, one of them pulled out a knife and stabbed his adversary and then ran away. People gathered around the injured man. He seemed to be lying still and may have been dead, we couldn't really tell. We informed the duty officer on the bridge, but there was nothing we could do. He just said we shouldn't get involved.

Seventy days after leaving Auckland, the bosun came to find me and told me I could stop work for an hour and go on deck.

I lent on the railings and looked out as the white cliffs of Dover came into view. It was an incredibly emotional sight and I could not tear my eyes away as they grew closer and larger. In my head, I hummed the tune, 'There'll be bluebirds over the white cliffs of Dover.' I looked round, I reckoned everyone else was doing the same.

I had been away for very nearly two years, but somehow, that walk up the corridor at Heathrow seemed like a lifetime ago.

The past few days had been interesting. I had been told the Bay of Biscay could be rough, and rough it was. The waves towered over the ship getting as high as the bridge and then crashing down, making a sound like the roar of thunder. I lay in my bed at night, tucked up and warm, listening to the sea but rather than making me feel nervous or afraid, it had the opposite effect. I felt safe and snug, it wasn't a bad life being a sailor. We moored in London docks and I said my goodbyes. I thanked the bosun who had looked out for me and been so kind and gave him a hug.

I declined Alfie and George's offer to be shown the highlights of Soho but agreed to swap addresses and telephone numbers. The ones I gave them were totally false. I boarded a taxi and, crammed in with five others, headed for Waterloo Station. Above the seat opposite was a sign saying:
Maximum number of passengers 4.

At the exit from the docks, a policeman flagged us down. A note was passed to him by the cabbie and we were on our way.

It was my only personal experience of an officer of the law being bribed.

Chapter 22　　Loose Ends

I played a trick on my parents and arrived on their doorstep a week before I was expected. I rang the bell and waited. My mum opened the door and looked blankly at me, probably wondering what a skinhead was doing bothering her. All of a sudden, the penny dropped. She screamed and gave me a ferocious hug. We were both in floods of tears. Thank heaven she didn't have a heart attack there and then.

When dad arrived home, he was equally pleased and excited. They plied me with questions for an hour. My brother Colin came in, said hi, sat down and read his newspaper as if I had only been gone for the afternoon. Mr Cool.

Dad told me he had great news. I had been accepted on a three year teaching course at the University of London Goldsmiths College. I had written to him months earlier and asked him to try and get me in. Colin had trained there and, in the past, mum dad and I had visited him several times and I loved New Cross and the area around. Dad said that the course comprised of teaching modules but also studying a main subject to degree level. I was so pleased until he said he had put me down for physics and mathematics. I was dumb struck; I felt like shouting at him, 'What on earth did you do that for.' Then I realised I was paying for the lie I told him about my A level results two years earlier.

In October, I headed to London to start my course. I attended ten physics and three maths lectures in the first few months and hardly understood anything. So, I simply stopped going.

I had a great year until the following May when I received a note from the dean of studies telling me to make an appointment to see him.

I went to his office the following day and he told me that I had failed the course and would not be taken back for a second year. He said how sad he was to do this as, in my teaching practice, I have been graded as outstanding. I asked if I could be given a second chance but he told me there was nothing he could do. Incredibly, I hadn't seen it coming. I was devastated.

Ironically, I was academic affairs vice president in the students union at the time and went to the union president, a wonderful man called Carl de Cruz, for help. He was furious with the college and went to see the dean immediately. The outcome was that I was allowed to start a new course the following year, doing either handicraft, PE or drama. I chose drama and had a wonderful three years. It led me to become a part time professional actor in a touring company for several years, and later, once I had retired as a teacher, appearing as an extra in many well known TV shows and films and, best of all, gain a love of drama and theatre, which remains to this day.

I was really sad when I heard that my friend Carl had died in 2010.

In my first teaching job at Kentwood School in Penge, I was able to set up my own drama department and direct many thoroughly enjoyable productions with staff, pupils and parents. It is strange indeed that I ended my career in a school in Somerset as head of maths. Odd how things work out.

When I first arrived back in England, I took Joseph's watch to a repair shop but was told it was cheap and not worth the bother. I had plenty of money from working my passage and bought him a new one. I sent it to him care of Giri Mission. Two years later I received a letter from Joseph accusing me of stealing his watch and breaking my promise. I was so upset. I bought him another one and sent it off. I never heard from him again despite writing several times. I have no idea if he received it. A sad ending to a great friendship. I hope it got there.

I have met a number of volunteers who really struggled to adjust to normal life even after many years. I was lucky I had a reasonable career and, on the whole, life has been good. On the other hand, I have never really done anything worthy of a newspaper front page. (If you don't count selling a piece of calcite to Kenneth Williams at Greenwich Market)

Except once.

In the months between getting back from New Guinea and starting college, I worked as a hod carrier on building sites. My first job was at a new school build, near Woking, working directly for the council. (I dare not say exactly where)

I have to say, compared with working for private companies, which I did later, it was quite laid back and not overtaxing.

In my first week, an old bricklayer named Joe told me to mix some mortar as he and his team were about to build a wall for a gymnasium. Expensive white bricks were going to be used, and it was going to look rather splendid.

"Mix the sand and cement and make sure you get the right ratio, one to six." He told me. Joe believed that work comprised of smoking, chatting, eating, drinking tea and a few bricks being laid if there was time. He wandered off to talk to a mate as I started loading the cement mixer. It occurred to me that he hadn't told me whether it was six sand and one cement or the other way round. I decided it had to be mostly cement, had to be, surely. By the end of the day, the wall was about seven feet high, and I suspected that was a world record for Joe and his fellow brickies in one day.

I arrived the following morning to find Joe staring at the wall.

"Here, young'un," he said, "this wall looks wrong to me; the mortar isn't the right colour. You did mix it one to six didn't you?"

"Yes," I said, "six cement to one sand."

His face went purple.

"Oh my God, it's supposed to be six sand to one cement." He followed this up with various comments about my parentage, intelligence, education, up bringing and size of brain. To be honest much of the vocabulary he used is not really suitable for a book such as this. He finished by saying.

"No offence!"

I was not offended; in fact, I was struggling not to laugh.

"Sorry," I said, trying to sound it, "will we have to start again?"

He thought for a minute, "No, bugger that, just make sure you don't tell anyone and mix it right from now on. I'm going for a smoke."

Seven years later, I was working in London and was on a train to Portsmouth to visit a friend. The chap sitting opposite me had boarded at Woking and when he got off at Petersfield, he left behind a copy of the Woking News and Mail. I picked it up and an article on the front page caught my eye.

The headline was-

Local School Gym White Wall Crumbles.

Council pays out tens of thousands of pounds for repairs.

<u>Gulp!</u>

Question
What has this got to do with New Guinea?

Answer
Nothing.

Part 2
Fifty Years On

Women

In New Guinea in 2020, there were over 15,000 incidents of domestic violence reported to the police but only 1.6% were investigated leading to an arrest. Only one third of those led to a conviction.

1.5 million people experienced gender-based violence and a woman was beaten every 30 seconds. It is probable that when COVID was prevalent, things were even worse.

These statistics include women who are attacked and even murdered because they are suspected of practising witchcraft or being witches.

It is estimated that around one in three women worldwide have been affected by violence at least once. In New Guinea, it is over two in three. Even more shocking is that over seven in every ten men feel it is justifiable for a husband to hit his wife.

In the late 60s, I doubt I had ever heard the term domestic violence, let alone looked out to see if it was happening. It may have been there, in Giri and in the other villages, but I never saw any physical abuse or violence between genders while in Papua New Guinea.

In this book, I've included a number of tales that I heard from a variety of people.

While writing them down from memory, I was surprised at the level of violence in many of them, often against women. At the time, it never occurred to me that it might reflect the reality of what may have been really happening locally. Most shocking were two stories that pupils in my class told. Both were boys and probably 13 to 15 years old.

It is not uncommon for a man to have more than one wife and in the first tale, a man wanted a younger wife. His first wife suspected that her role would end up having to do all the cooking and cleaning. She vehemently objected, refused to do any of her normal work and also made up and spread lies about the new woman.

In the second, the married couple were older and the wife was well known in her village for nagging; she was forever telling her husband how useless he was at everything and moaning about her life.

Both women suffered the same fate. Their husbands and their accomplices tied them by their feet and hung them from a high branch in a tree. One was naked and, when released, was so ashamed she ran into the bush and was never seen again. The other was left for a week and was already dead when she was cut down.

There is no doubt in my mind that these boys had not seen this happen but had heard the stories from an adult. They were certainly not made up on the spot. It is possible, I suppose, that they had really happened.

As a boy, I remember seeing Punch and Judy shows at the seaside which were incredibly misogynistic. I didn't make a link between the show and reality, but perhaps some would.

The truth is, I don't know if domestic violence happened in Giri in 1968. I hope not, but if it did, it would have happened with the whole community knowing about it.

From the beginning of my stay, I felt uneasy with the difference in treatment between men and women in Giri and all the other villages.

When I first arrived, I saw a man and his wife returning to the village from their garden; the man in front and the woman a few paces behind, which turned out to be the norm. She had a huge bag of firewood on her back hanging from a strap around her forehead. Attached to that was another bag full of yams and other vegetables and perched right at the top was a baby. The man, strolling in front, carried a small axe. At the time, it seemed so alien to me.

Perhaps this behaviour was a form of domestic violence. The woman would have been brought up learning that that was the correct way to behave as it had been for hundreds of years. But if she refused?

When my parents went out together, my dad would never allow Mum to carry anything heavy, nor walk some paces behind.

In Giri, there were definite tasks that were nearly always done by men and others by women. I rarely saw a man cleaning or looking after a baby, nor did they collect firewood or water. Women did not hunt or build. Cooking was usually done by the women but not always. The older boys who stayed in the school boarding house never seemed to mind cooking.

The ritual involved in Sing Sings was carried out by men and the feast would involve the men eating first and women and children later. The best of the pig meat would always go to the men, and women ended up with the less salubrious parts. In some families the men ate before the rest of the family but that was not always the case. Joseph and Abi's family all ate together. Others did the same.

When I became an established visitor to Giri, I tried to persuade the people with influence in the village to allow women in the meeting house. They always said no and gave the same reasons; firstly, it was the tradition that women were not allowed in, going back as long as could be remembered, and secondly, single men slept in the place, which made it inappropriate for women to enter. I talked to Joseph about it and he thought they were being honest and he wasn't aware of any taboo involved.

Gradually I managed to get people on my side, and by the time my year was coming to a close, they relented, probably just to get me off their backs. Only for village meetings, but at least it was a start. And so, one June evening at a village gathering, three women, including Abi, entered for the first time. I felt very proud and pleased for them.

Months later I asked my successor, Jim, if they were still allowed in. He didn't think they were. I remember hoping that girls and boys mixing at school might eventually break down barriers.

A village woman carrying a huge and very heavy net of firewood.

Published with kind permission of

Sacred Land Film Project

Posted August 2019

On the Ramu River in Papua New Guinea, the Songnor have thrived for 6000 years living in grass huts on stilts, dependent on the river, forest and household gardens for sustenance. In Bosmun Village and upriver in Kurumbukari, the Songnor catch fish in hand-woven traps, white and purple yams are dug from dark soil, and edible starch is laboriously extracted from the sago palm. The village is surrounded by incredible biological diversity, with tree kangaroos, orchids and birds of paradise seen nowhere else in the world.

Papua New Guinea is not only rich in biological resources, however. Described as "an island of gold in a sea of oil," Papua New Guinea's mineral wealth and petroleum reserves have drawn scores of international mining companies in a rush to stake their claim on the landscape.

Indigenous people living along the Ramu River fear that runoff from the ongoing construction of the massive Chinese government-owned Ramu NiCo mine will poison their water, fish and gardens and destroy their environment. Those along the coast worry about the mine waste being dumped at sea and its effect on their health and fisheries.

Says Melchior Ware, village elder and clan leader of Bosmun village, "The land has always been a communal property for the people. We are the only guardians. We have a different perspective. We are guardians of the land. We belong to this land, it is our source. We, in return, regard the land, the environment, and the river as sacred because they

206

provide to us life. If you're going to cut off the very source of life, we are most likely to fight-and we will fight."

The Land and Its People

Papua New Guinea occupies the eastern half of the Melanesian island of New Guinea and several smaller islands. The country's motto, "unity in diversity," is apt: it is one of the most ethnically and biologically diverse countries in the world.

Some 60 percent of this mountainous land is covered by tropical forest, representing, along with neighbouring West Papua, the world's third-largest intact rainforest. The forests contain an estimated 5 to 7 percent of the world's biodiversity. A country just shy of 6.5 million people, it also possesses a wealth of natural resources beneath its largely non-arable land.

There are more than 800 indigenous languages spoken by the people of Papua New Guinea and a stunning range of cultural diversity. Most people live in small communities, where they practise subsistence farming and depend on the forests, rivers and sea to provide their food, water, medicine and building materials. Eighty-Five percent of the residents continue to live off the land.

Rather than being bought and sold, land is passed down through generations, and it is a source of identity and spiritual connection as well as survival. Ninety-seven percent of the land in Papua New Guinea is under legally recognised customary-land title, meaning that the country's indigenous people have rightful ownership of the traditional lands they occupy.

The Ramu River begins in the Kratke Range and runs almost 400 miles to the Bismarck Sea in northern Papa New Guinea. Though largely unnavigable, the

Ramu River is home to the Dumpu, Bundi, Atemble settlements, among others. Located on top of a rich mineral deposit, Kurumbukari village was once home to about 1000 people. Kurumbukari Villagers have lived in the area for 6500 years and regard the Ramu river as sacred because of its vital role in sustaining their traditional way of life in addition to being their primary source of food and water.

The Mining Threat

Begun in 2008, the Ramu Nico nickel and cobalt mining project in northeastern Papua New Guinea consists of three parts:

the Kurumbukari mine sites, the Basanuk refinery, and the 135 km pipeline that transports slurry from the mine site to the refinery located on the coast. Once the nickel and cobalt are extracted at the refinery, the waste-including arsenic, copper, chromium, cadmium, mercury and high levels of ammonia- are pumped through another pipeline and dumped 150 metres deep into Bismarck Bay.

The mine is owned by China Metallurgical Group Corporation (MCC) and is expected to operate for 35-40 years. The company claimed the mine "showcases the strong commitment of the (mining) company in building sustainability and mutuality for both the Project and the local community," which led some local residents to see it as a potential boon, offering medical and educational infrastructure to their remote villages. That opinion changed once they realised the scope and impact of the enormous project.

The village of Kurumbukari sat on top of the mineral riches, so China Metallurgical Group Corporation gave the residents a week to move out, spray-painting "Out" on their homes. The company offered them $230 to move to Snake Mountain, but that area is considered taboo, traditionally off-limits to any activity. For people who are so connected to the land, this was unacceptable, making them "feel like animals." Those few who stayed were forcibly removed; their houses destroyed before their eyes.

Despite legal challenges, the mine is in operation. Erosion run-off degrades water quality and has destroyed traditional fishing grounds downstream. An even greater concern is the potential contamination of their food supply. Along the river people depend on river flooding to irrigate their yam and sweet potato crops. Heavy metals and other pollutants running downstream from the mine could destroy this critical food source or make it inedible.

At the Basamuk refinery, Sama Mellombo, a clan leader of a village near the refinery, is outraged that the mining company destroyed his clan's cemetery in violation of the explicit instructions of their permit. The company suffered no consequences for this illegal activity.

The people along the coast near the refinery are dependent on Bismarck Bay for fishing, bathing, salt and medicine. They were concerned about pollution threats from the tailings to be dumped into the sea. The theory behind deep water disposal is that the mine waste, which is denser then seawater, will sink to the seabed and stay put. But the theory discounts the likelihood of currents and upwelling bringing the pollution into shallow water and dispersing it, compromising the health of the marine environment. This waste includes arsenic, copper, chromium, cadmium, mercury and high levels of ammonia.

The government hired scientists to assess potential harm to marine life. When the scientists warned that the damage could be widespread, it suppressed and ignored their findings. Later, when coastal landowner clans sued over the mining company's "deep submarine tailings placement," which would dump 14,000 tons of toxic waste per day into the Bay, the government passed a law that denies citizens the right to appeal any permit granted by the Department of Environment and Conservation, regardless of its impact on health livelihoods and culture.

With Bismarck Ramu Group, a community organising collective, Sama Mellamba and Melchior Ware allied with other local leaders, filed lawsuits to stop construction of the mine and dumping of waste into the sea. Outraged by the backroom deals, inequitable compensation and irreversible impacts on land and water, landowners who have only recently been introduced to the cash economy are now banding together to protect their traditional lands and sacred places from development by major multinational corporations. So far, they have had little effect. The mine and deep sea dumping continue unabated.

https://sacredland.org/ramu-river-papua-new-guinea/
https://sacredland.org/join

New Guinea was discovered by the Portuguese explorer Don Jorge de Meneses In 1512. It has been inhabited for at least five thousand years. The diversity of cultures and the fact that over eight hundred different languages have been spoken over the years suggests there was wave upon wave of immigration. Over the years, Pidgin English (tok pisin) has been introduced to many areas and is an official language. New Guinea is the second largest island in the world, the largest being Greenland. It gained its independence from Australia in 1975.

I would like to thank and dedicate this book to all the following people.

My wife **Sue**; motivator and corrector of grammer and spelings.

Author **Carmel Doohan** for her advice and help.

My kids; **Jen** for her constant encouragement. **James** for working out the complexities of numbering pages in Microsoft Word. **Pete** for designing the amazing cover. **Kate** for reading the first draft to her friends on holiday which they all enjoyed. A real boost to my confidence.

Jim McManus and **Sheila Glasswell** for allowing me to use their photographs and for sharing their memories.

The fabulous women of the Cheddar Writers Group; **Jenny**, **Jude**, **Angela**, **Sally**, **Margaret**, **Heather** and our leader, **Sue Purkiss**; author of many brilliant children's books, for their inspiration, support and honest opinions.

Voluntary Service Overseas for the truly amazing opportunity they gave me and thousands of others and especially **Heidi** for finding Jim.

Dave at **JD&J Design LLC** for formatting the cover so efficiently.

But most of all, the beautiful people of **Giri**, **Arengin** and all the other mission villages.

Joseph, Abi, Peter and Ruth Hurri

with Grandpa and Cousins

All photographs apart from those labelled, were taken between 1968 and 1971 by Richard Masters, Jim McManus, Sheila Glasswell or others present at the time.

Many of the photographs are in colour in the hardback version of the book.

Also available from Amazon.

Printed in Great Britain
by Amazon

28109031R10126